SELF-DOUBT
DETOX

5 Steps
to Beat Your
Bully and Bloom
Confidence

TREVA GRAVES, M.A.

Self-Doubt Detox:
5 Steps to Beat Your Bully and Bloom Confidence
by Treva Graves

Copyright © 2023 by Treva Graves

All Rights Reserved. No part of this publication may be reproduced, stored in a retrieval system, or transmitted in any form or by any means, electronic, mechanical, photocopying, recording, scanning, or otherwise, without the prior written permission of the author.

ISBN (paperback) 979-8-3920-3713-1
ISBN (hardcover) 978-1-0881-0232-9
Also available as an e-book

Editing by Shannon Dunn, Editing Insights
Cover and interior design by DTPerfect Book Design

www.bloompersonalbranding.com

Table of Contents

DEDICATION vii
FOREWORD ix
INTRODUCTION 1
    How To Read This Book 3
CHAPTER ONE GET TO KNOW YOUR BULLY 7
    School-Aged Bully 7
    Workplace Bully 9
    Spouse/Partner Bully 11
    Toxic Friend Bully 15
    Family Bully 16
    Yourself (Imposter Syndrome) Bully 17
    Addiction Bully 19
CHAPTER TWO SELF-DOUBT 25
    Activity #1 – Look For Themes 32
    Activity #2 – Self-Doubt Quiz 33
    Develop Intention 36
CHAPTER THREE BELIEVE 39
    Seven Ways To Believe in Yourself 46
    Positive Affirmations 47

Activity #3 – Self-Assessment: Accept and Believe in
Your Strengths 50

Activity #4 – Five-Minute Confidence 52

CHAPTER FOUR LOVE YOURSELF 55

12 Self-Love Ideas 62

Key Takeaways 66

Activity #5 – Self-Assessment – Where Are You in Your
Self-Love Journey? 67

CHAPTER FIVE OBSERVATION 71

Benefits of Observation 72

Albert Bandura's 4 Stages of Observational Learning 74

Body Language 75

Activity #6 – Observational Learning 77

Activity #7 – Wear Something That Makes You Feel
Confident 78

CHAPTER SIX OPPORTUNITIES 81

Nine Tips To Help You Seize Every Opportunity 83

Activity #8 – Take Advantage of a New Opportunity 89

CHAPTER SEVEN MENTOR 91

The Three A's of Mentorship 93

Activity #9 – Ten Professional Mentoring Activities To
Consider 96

Questions To Ask a Mentor 97

Successful Mentoring Sessions 98

CHAPTER EIGHT SELF-WORTH 101

What Is the Meaning of Self-Worth and Self-Value? 104

What Determines Self-Worth? 104

TABLE OF CONTENTS

    Activity #10 – Develop Your Self-Worth 108
    Self-Worth Worksheet 113
    My Strengths and Qualities Worksheet 114
    Meditations To Boost Self-Worth. 116
    30-Day Journal Activity. 116
    Powerful Women Playlist 117
CONCLUSION **119**
    BLOOM Methodology Key Takeaways 121
RESOURCES. **123**

Dedication

I dedicate this book to all the mentors in my life who saw a strength in me I didn't. Thank you for showing me it's okay to be myself and challenging me to share my voice with the world. You have left footprints in my life forever.

Foreword

As a Champion for Change, I have spent over two decades in self-examination, higher education and working with people globally who are seekers. These individuals are always searching for knowledge, wisdom and techniques to bring their gifts to all humanity. I believe human beings should live healthy, fulfilled and purpose-driven lives. A huge component of achieving that vision is based on building self-confidence.

When you feel confident, you feel everything in life is going your way. Your job is great, you are happy in your relationships, and all is well in your mind, body and soul. But when self-doubt creeps in, your life can change in an instant and spiral downward. There are many things that perpetuate your self-doubt, including trauma, bullies and fear. Have you ever wondered how you can move through self-doubt into self-confidence? Well, you're not alone. Most people struggle with insecurities at some point in their lives and seek help.

Treva Graves spent her childhood and young adult life stuck in self-doubt and insecurity. This led her to seek help. She became determined to defeat it and wanted to develop intention and belief in herself to overcome these crippling feelings. In this book, Treva shares traumatic experiences and challenges she faced on her journey to self-confidence. She went from being bullied in a small town in South Dakota to becoming a crowned beauty queen on a world-class stage—and so much more. Treva Graves gives you the gift of her branded BLOOM Methodology to help you take back your power from your inner bully and live the life you always wanted.

Cynthia James is a transformational specialist and one of today's brightest and best loved inspirational leaders and teachers guiding thousands of people to make changes at a deep level for lasting healing in their lives. She is a bestselling author of three award-winning books, "What Will Set You Free," "Revealing Your Extraordinary Essence" and "I Choose Me: The Art of Being A Phenomenally Successful Woman at Home and at Work." Her current book, "Does My Voice Matter," shares her journey of self-discovery, authenticity and empowerment. https://cynthiajames.net

Introduction

In a world where we've been force-fed from a young age a constantly changing form of what "normal" or "perfect" should look like, with many of us believing we don't fit into this mold, being comfortable as ourselves never stood a chance. Add to that our deep-rooted cultural behavior of self-deprecation and we're left with an unhealthy mindset. Not only are we convinced that we don't fit in, but we compound the problem by putting ourselves down because of it.

Being rejected by peers or even family at an early age can make you carry an "outsider" identity for years afterward. As an adult, you might avoid engaging with others for fear of rejection, or you might swing to the other extreme and become overly concerned with being perfect. The need to be perfect drives unrealistically high expectations where you focus on your flaws and missteps. Don't let "I am not good enough" lead you to a path that jeopardizes your health and relationships.

We can trace a persistent feeling of not measuring up to over-critical parents, bullying from classmates or a tendency to compare ourselves to others. This belief can lead us to push ourselves too hard to overcompensate. I know this was true for me, as I felt I had to be perfect, successful and educated to be taken seriously. However, it can also cause Imposter Syndrome. This affects people who see themselves as failures, and women suffer from it at a much higher level than men. If you are currently experiencing feelings of self-doubt and thinking you are not good enough, you are not alone.

Despite what we see on the outside, most people battle feelings of inadequacy and question their self-worth daily. Did you know research shows that most people don't feel fully confident until they are 60 years old? Whether you are a world-famous actress, CEO or working mom navigating the challenges of life, self-confidence may seem elusive no matter how much you achieve. Self-doubt is much more common than we'd like to admit, but you can learn to change the negative self-talk and stop feeling small.

You may have had a bully in your life at some point. Your bully could be your boss, a co-worker, a spouse, or even a toxic friend. Your bully may not even be a person. Bullies come in all shapes, forms and sizes. Maybe your bully is an imposter that sits in your brain telling you that you can't do something or will fail. Thousands of women want to start businesses, leave unhappy relationships or move into a leadership position but lack the self-confidence to do it. I was one of those women.

My journey to detox my self-doubt took me a while, but that's okay. Everyone is different. I spent most of my childhood stuck in self-doubt and insecurity. I was severely bullied as a child, had few friends and never really fit in. Throughout my life, I experienced more bullying in different ways, and I suffered from low self-esteem. I craved to look and feel confident, like the women I read about in books, saw in magazines and television and observed in executive positions.

When I dug deeper into the lives of those successful women, I realized that many of their stories did not differ from mine. This inspired me, and I decided I needed a Self-Doubt Detox to gain confidence and feel better about myself. I tried to do it on my own but failed many times. I finally worked with a personal coach, long before coaches were mainstream, and she helped me improve my life and move forward toward my goals.

Today, I am a personal branding expert, author and speaker. I own a successful coaching and corporate training company, Bloom Personal Branding. I inspire people to build self-confidence and

INTRODUCTION

reach their goals. Since 2013, I coached hundreds of clients to build influence, impact, credibility, and income by creating powerful personal brands. My list of clients includes seven-figure entrepreneurs, New York Times bestselling authors, professional speakers, coaches, politicians, start-up entrepreneurs, leaders, and business and sales professionals.

Because of the challenges and triumphs I experienced, I have a deep passion for helping women achieve their goals. I wrote this book to share my personal experiences, both good and bad, to show you exactly what I did to get where I am today. I believe in myself. I have more confidence. I am successful. I create long-lasting relationships. I live a happier, more productive life.

I will teach you how to overcome the roadblocks you face by using my branded BLOOM Methodology. These 5 steps to beat your bully and bloom confidence are simple and practical strategies you can quickly and easily apply wherever you are in your self-confidence journey. As you build your self-confidence with the tools provided in this book, remember you're building a stronger relationship with yourself!

Believe
Love Yourself
Observation
Opportunities
Mentor

HOW TO READ THIS BOOK

In this book, I show you how to begin exploring the root causes of your feelings and discover what is influencing your self-confidence so you can become inspired to act and find the motivation to work toward a healthy mindset. I also show you how to listen to your gut feelings, discover what you truly want then how to achieve what you discover.

In Chapter One, I explain the different types of bullies and how they may have impacted your life. This can help you identify, acknowledge and validate your experiences, which is an essential part of your Self-Doubt Detox. You may be allowing these people, events and circumstances to hold you back from your bright and positive future.

In Chapters Two through Seven, I share my personal experiences, both positive and negative, to show you exactly what I did to start living a fulfilling life. Then, I teach how you can detox your self-doubt using my BLOOM Methodology. These exercises, tips and guidance can help you learn how to leave your bully behind and become more confident.

In Chapter Eight, I show you how to reclaim your voice and realize its value. Most importantly, I give you the tools to become bold and brave enough to access the power within you to achieve your goals and create a positive mindset to live the life you deserve.

In conclusion, I summarize my journey of Self-Doubt Detox, share key points from my BLOOM Methodology and provide you with the motivation you need to continue your Self-Doubt Detox to Beat Your Bully and Bloom Confidence.

As I always say to my clients, *"Success in anything isn't a matter of circumstance. It's a matter of choice."*

The journey to self-discovery and self-confidence takes work and commitment, but you can move forward in a positive direction and live life on your terms. You have the power within you to live your dreams.

You are in charge of your thinking and responsible for your actions and outcomes. When you are willing to make a meaningful change in your behavior each day to become more confident, your positive results can be permanent. Now let's get started together on *your* Self-Doubt Detox!

*If you give your power to the bully,
the bully always wins.*
TREVA GRAVES

CHAPTER One
Get to Know Your Bully

It's so important to understand what bullying is and how it affects you.

Bullying is the abuse and mistreatment of someone vulnerable by someone stronger and more powerful. The behavior is repeated or has the potential to repeat over time. Bullies can be people or anything that impacts your life negatively and diminishes your self-worth.

As you learn about the different types of bullies, see which ones you identify with. You may recognize that you have more than one bully. I've certainly had my share. Your bully may be from your childhood, recent past or present. I want you to circle any information here that relates to your feelings or experiences with your bully.

SCHOOL-AGED BULLY

School-aged bullying is among the most common type. Bullying can start as early as kindergarten, occur during or after school hours and happen anywhere. While most reported bullying happens in the school building, a significant percentage also happens on the playground or bus. It can also occur traveling to or from school, in the youth's neighborhood or on the Internet. Did you know that over one million children have admitted to being bullied on Facebook?

Three Main Types of School-Aged Bullying

1. **Verbal Bullying** is saying or writing mean things including teasing, name-calling, inappropriate sexual comments, taunting, and threatening to cause harm.

2. **Social and Cyber Bullying** can be in person and/or online/social media or online gaming involving hurting someone's reputation or relationships. This includes purposely excluding someone, telling other children not to be friends with someone, spreading rumors, or embarrassing them in public.

3. **Physical Bullying** involves hurting a person's body or possessions by hitting, kicking, pinching, spitting, tripping, pushing, and taking or breaking someone's things. Making mean or rude hand gestures is also considered physical bullying.

Effects of School-Aged Bullying

Kids who are bullied are more likely to miss, skip or drop out of school, experience a dramatic decrease in academic achievement, and lose interest in school activities. They can experience depression and anxiety, increased feelings of sadness and loneliness, and changes in sleep and eating patterns. These issues can carry into adulthood and negatively impact their quality of life. In many cases, bullying is linked to suicide. The risk of suicide is especially high for American Indian, Alaskan Native, Asian American, and LGQBTQ2S+ youth. Kids who are bullied must be supported by parents, peers and schools. It's essential to keep open communication with kids, check in on their mental health, ask questions and listen to their concerns to uncover any bullying they may be

CHAPTER ONE   GET TO KNOW YOUR BULLY

experiencing. For more information on bullying, go to stopbullying.gov.

WORKPLACE BULLY

Co-Worker Bully

Bullying doesn't end with school. It often carries into the workplace. In 2021, a study by workplacebullying.org revealed 25% of respondents said they had felt bullied by a peer or co-worker. Women bully women twice as much as they bully men. The study also showed that 35% of Hispanics are bullied more than any other race. Workplace bullying takes on many forms, like having your work stolen or sabotaged, being humiliated or being ostracized.

Since Covid-19, there has been an increase in remote work, and employees are experiencing a new type of bullying as it's easier to bully people when they don't have to see them face to face. This new bullying is hidden behind instant messenger chats and text messages. The casual home office often leads employees to act less professionally than they would in their organization's physical office. They are more likely to drop their guard about what they say and do via email, messaging and video-conference platforms.

Examples of Remote and In-Office Bullying

- Messages containing sexist or discriminatory remarks
- Threatening messages or emails
- Demeaning, belittling or talking over someone during meetings or video calls
- Micromanaging every detail of work an employee does
- Spreading gossip or rumors about co-workers
- Taking credit for someone else's work

9

- Withholding the necessary resources for someone to get their job done
- Gaslighting and making an employee second guess themselves

Boss Bully

Many times, people do not realize their boss is bullying them. Instead, they believe they have a tough boss or one that simply pushes their employees to get results. It's interesting to note that 65% of adult bullies are bosses, which is one of the most difficult situations. It is imperative to be able to identify a boss bully because your boss is the person who decides your future within the company.

Signs Your Boss Is a Bully

Impeding your success is one way a boss can bully you. They may make it impossible for you to apply for a promotion, a transfer or additional training. They may even manipulate you with promises of promotions or raises to get you to work extra hours—then never deliver on those promises. Boss bullies can stop your success by excluding you from company outings, social events or after-hours meetings. They may also schedule meetings when they know you are on vacation or have a conflict.

A bullying boss might threaten to physically harm you. They may tower over you, invade your space and give intimidating looks. They may also intimidate you by threatening to fire you to maintain power and control or verbally abuse and humiliate you by shouting or swearing at you privately or publicly. Offensive jokes at your expense or giving unfair criticism are also ways of bullying.

Intruding on your privacy by spying on you or stalking you is bullying. Employers may listen in on your private conversations, open your mail or tamper with your personal belongings or work equipment. It's common to find a bullying boss snooping through your office when you are out. Ultimately, they are looking for ammunition to use against you.

CHAPTER ONE GET TO KNOW YOUR BULLY

Bosses that bully question your ability by belittling your opinions and ideas. This behavior may take place privately or publicly. A bullying boss may also question your commitment to the job if you don't work long hours and sacrifice personal time. Even then, you likely can never do enough to please them. They may undermine your work by setting unrealistic deadlines that are bound to cause failure.

Why Workplace Bullying is Harmful

Often, employees will endure bullying and poor treatment from their co-workers and bosses simply because they're afraid of being fired or creating a tense situation. Workplace bullying can lead to health concerns, undue stress, low productivity, and impede career advancement. It will probably continue if you never address it. If you are at the point where you feel like you're walking on eggshells, being taken advantage of, or you are feeling anxious, sad, or frightened, then it may be time to stand up to workplace bullying. Take the appropriate steps to handle bullying at work to support your overall well-being by consulting with your human resources department or a lawyer.

SPOUSE/PARTNER BULLY

We typically think bullies are primarily acquaintances from school or the workplace or complete strangers who feel good when bullying others. We are less likely to believe our loved ones could be bullies, but bullying behavior *can* occur in close relationships. There are many motivations for spouse bullying. Many bullies cover up their own feelings of inadequacy and low self-esteem by putting others down. Some bullies are egocentric, narcissistic and uncaring about the impact of their behavior on others. Some spouse bullies were themselves targets of bullies or may get bullied at work and bring it home.

Being married to a bully can lead to stress and anxiety and may be an early warning of physical abuse. In the United States, over ten million adults experience domestic violence annually from spouse bullies. That said, bullying doesn't always manifest as physical violence. If your partner is a bully, he/she may try to coerce or force you into compliance or even intimidate you and your children with an aggressive tone or threats.

Signs Your Spouse/Partner Is a Bully

1. **Name-Calling:** This is typical bullying behavior. Often the names are simply negative (e.g., profane, such as "bitch/bastard" or worse) but may also take the form of belittling labels (i.e., "stupid," "idiot," etc.).

2. **Taunting:** When you try to stand up to your spouse's or partner's verbal (or physical) attacks, the bully taunts you, both as a put-down and as a means of controlling you (e.g., "What are you going to do about it?" "Go ahead, call the cops. Who's going to believe you?").

3. **Verbal and Physical Aggression:** Besides name-calling, a bully can go off on verbal tirades and may get physically (or sexually) aggressive. Obviously, aggressive attacks are serious and are often the triggers to seeking help or getting out of the relationship. If your spouse or partner becomes physically aggressive or is using a weapon, you need to leave immediately.

4. **Controlling Behavior:** Over-controlling and not allowing a spouse any freedom or autonomy is bullying. I endured this behavior almost daily with my ex-husband. Constant criticizing and put-downs ("Can't you do anything right?" "You're doing it wrong!") make the spouse feel small and emphasize the bully's imagined superiority.

5. **Put Downs in Front of Others:** Publicly belittling a spouse or partner to others is another bullying behavior ("Let me tell you how stupid she is."). Another way the bully dominates is to expose the spouse's secrets in a negative way ("She really wants to be the manager at work. Can you imagine that?").

CHAPTER ONE GET TO KNOW YOUR BULLY

What To Do If You Are Married to a Bully

Some partners live in denial of their spouses' bullying tactics because they don't want to confront the issue. However, without intervention, this behavior will most likely continue. Seek counseling and keep a journal to document your feelings and cite specific occurrences. Take pictures if there is physical abuse involved. Stop making excuses for their bad behavior regardless of how many good times you've had together. Quit taking it, or they will continue to bully you. Set boundaries for how you want to be treated and leave if those boundaries are violated. If your spouse is a bully, you deserve better. If you have kids, *they* deserve better. Bullying takes on an even bigger consequence when children are involved. Research shows that children growing up in a home with a bullying parent are more likely to become bullies or be bullied themselves. Make a choice to end the cycle of bullying.

A Safety Plan

Creating a safety plan for leaving an abusive relationship can be vital for successfully breaking free and survival. Below are some suggestions of things you can do to prepare yourself.

- **Finances** – Having finances to rely on (that your bully doesn't have access to) is a must to ensure your survival outside of the relationship. Start putting money aside as you formulate your plan.

- **Phone** – If you have a bully who is very controlling of your phone and social life, it will be best for you to make purchasing a "burner" phone a priority.

- **Work** – Giving your workplace a heads-up and having a plan in place for your work when you leave will alleviate a lot of stress. This will allow your mind to focus on the tasks you'll have to complete when you leave. The goal is to hopefully not lose your job or financial stability when you leave the relationship so that you can survive on your own without your abuser.

- **Housing** – The BIGGEST problem victims run into when leaving an abusive relationship is where they will live. Where will their kids live? Housing costs should be less than 30% of your monthly income, but when you have been sharing those costs with another person, it makes it difficult to figure out how you will survive on your own. Also, make sure that you are taking care of your possessions as well. Consider a shelter if you are financially challenged or in fear for your immediate safety.

- **Rely on Family and Friends** – You may have lost some by this point, but that doesn't mean they won't try to help you. Reach out. Help is necessary, especially if kids are involved. Your bully is likely to contact them to try and find out where you are and won't be above lying or threatening to get information. Keep your plan confidential and your circle of support small.

- **Support** – Consider working with a shelter or therapist on your plan. You'll likely benefit from counseling as you make these changes. You will especially want that extra support for any children involved.

By now, you should have money in your accounts and a new phone. You should have arrangements for your kids in place, your irreplaceable belongings should be safe elsewhere and you should know exactly where you are headed once you close the door on this chapter of your life.

Once You Are Out

The bully is the most dangerous when they realize they have lost control of their possession (you). These safety precautions are essential. The bully will try anything and everything, even suicide threats, to get your attention. Don't fall for the games. The bully will try anything to regain control.

CHAPTER ONE GET TO KNOW YOUR BULLY

TOXIC FRIEND BULLY

Friendship bullying is a friend who bullies another friend. Sometimes adults call this "relational bullying" since it happens within a relationship between two people. No matter what you call it, this is bullying. This type of bullying can happen to anyone, at any age, from kids just starting school to teenagers and adults. That's right—even adults can experience bullying from a friend.

Friendship bullying has many similarities with regular bullying, but because it happens within a friendship group or between friends, the person being bullied may think it's a normal part of having friends. It can be challenging for someone to distinguish between playful back-and-forth talk or bullying, especially if the friend says, "It was just a joke" or "Can't you take it?"

Three Ways a Friend Is a Bully

1. **Control:** They exercise power over who you should be friends with and deciding what to do and where to go without considering your feelings

2. **Manipulation:** They ask for and expect your help but don't ever have time to help you.

3. **Sabotage:** They don't want you to succeed or have more or better than they have. They discourage you from applying for your dream job or going out with someone great.

If a friend does any of the things listed, they are not your friend. Look for new people who will value your time and friendship and want the best for you!

FAMILY BULLY

Family bullying can have a lasting negative impact. Adults who are bullied experience many physical and mental consequences as a result. For instance, 71% of family bullying targets reported struggling with stress, 70% indicated that depression and anxiety were a concern, and 55% reported a loss in confidence. Other effects of adult bullying included sleep loss, headaches, muscle tension, and pain. The emotional strain caused by adult bullying could even lead to gastrointestinal changes, elevated blood pressure and cardiovascular issues.

Warning Signs of Family Bullying

Adult bullying tactics are more subtle, manipulative and controlling than those children use. Bullying tends to happen more slowly over time through small actions and words. Experiencing this type of behavior can be confusing and cause you to doubt your perceptions. You may even question your memory or your judgment. It can be helpful to write down bullying incidents, including how they made you feel. Doing so will help you recognize that what you're experiencing is real and not something you're imagining. Recognizing the signs of bullying involves looking at how your interactions with the other person make you feel. If you feel hurt, confused, frustrated, misunderstood, anxious, or worthless any time you interact with this person, chances are high that you're being bullied.

A family member who is bullying you may have unrealistic expectations or make unreasonable demands, blame you when things go wrong and invalidate your thoughts and feelings by undermining, minimizing or dismissing you. They create chaos in your life by starting arguments, nitpicking or making contradictory statements. They may use emotional blackmail to control you or make you feel guilty and act superior or condescending and try to prove you're wrong. They may even accuse you of being selfish, needy or not committed to the family and give you the silent treatment or attempt to get other family members to turn against you or shun you.

CHAPTER ONE GET TO KNOW YOUR BULLY

Impact

If these things are happening in your family, it's normal to feel that your power is being diminished. You may also feel like your emotional or mental health is suffering because of the bullying. If that is the case, it's time to start questioning the health of the relationship. Not only should you consider limiting your contact with this family member, but you may also want to get outside help, such as a counselor or a mental health professional, to help you learn how to interact and cope with this family member.

YOURSELF (IMPOSTER SYNDROME) BULLY

Have you ever felt like you've only succeeded due to luck and not because of your talent or qualifications? Do you worry that your friends or colleagues will discover you're a fraud and you don't deserve your job and accomplishments? If so, you're in good company. These feelings are known as Imposter Syndrome. An estimated 85% of women experience imposter feelings at some point in their lives. Imposter Syndrome can affect all men and women from all parts of life and careers.

Why Do People Experience Imposter Syndrome?

There's no single answer. Some experts believe it has to do with personality traits—like anxiety or neuroticism—while others focus on family or behavioral causes. Sometimes childhood memories, such as feeling that your grades were never good enough for your parents or that your siblings outshone you in certain areas, can leave a lasting impact.

Five Patterns of People Who Experience Imposter Feelings

Imposter Syndrome expert Valerie Young, who is the author of a book on the subject, "The Secret Thoughts of Successful Women," has found five patterns in people who experience imposter feelings:

1. **"Perfectionists"** set extremely high expectations for themselves, and even if they meet 99% of their goals, they're going to feel like failures. Any small mistake will make them question their own competence.

2. **"Experts"** feel the need to know every piece of information before they start a project and constantly look for new certifications or training to improve their skills. They won't apply for a job if they don't meet all the criteria in the posting and might be hesitant to ask a question in class or speak up at a meeting at work because they're afraid of looking stupid because they don't already know the answer.

3. **"Natural geniuses"** struggle or work hard to accomplish something because they think this means they aren't good enough. They are used to skills coming easily, and when they have to put in the effort, their brain tells them that's proof they're an imposter.

4. **"Soloists"** feel they must accomplish tasks on their own, and if they need to ask for help, they think that means they are a failure or a fraud.

5. **"Supermen" or "Superwomen"** push themselves to work harder than those around them to prove that they're not imposters. They feel the need to succeed in all aspects of life—at work, as parents, as partners—and may feel stressed when they are not accomplishing something.

How To Deal With An Imposter Syndrome Bully

Learn to value constructive criticism, ask for help and remember that the more you practice a skill, the better you will get at it. Acknowledge the thoughts and put them in perspective. Ask yourself, 'Does that thought help or hinder me?' It can also be helpful to share what you're feeling with trusted friends or mentors. People with more experience can reassure you that what you're feeling is normal, and knowing others have been in your position can make it seem less scary. Most people experience moments of doubt, and that's normal. The important part is not to let that doubt control your actions. If you want to delve more deeply into these feelings, consider seeking out a professional psychologist.

ADDICTION BULLY

Now, some of you may be surprised that I have included addictions as bullies, but I see them as bullies, too. They prey on creating low self-esteem and low self-value to prevent you from being the person you are meant to be. Most people understand addiction when it comes to dependence on substances, such as alcohol, nicotine, illicit drugs, or even prescription medications, but they have a hard time with the concept of addictive behaviors. Some activities are so normal that it's hard to believe people can become addicted to them. Yet the cycle of addiction can still take over, making everyday life a constant struggle, and people find it even harder to have self-confidence as their addiction bully covers up who they truly are. These behaviors could be personified as bullies because they rob your confidence just as much or even more than the previous bullies I've shared with you.

What Does Personification Mean?

My friend, Dr. Lyn Shroyer, licensed psychologist, explains the concept of personification like this: "Personification is used to give human traits and characteristics, such as emotions and behaviors, to non-human things, animals, or ideas. It's as if a human voice is talking to you and telling you to do something."

Common Addiction Bullies

Alcohol

The alcohol bully could be personified as a bottle of vodka that acts as a "mean girl" sitting in your liquor cabinet who starts out as your friend but knows all your vulnerabilities. That's when she'll kick you in the ass and drag you down. Think of it like this: You are at a party, and you take a drink of your Shirley Temple with good intentions of having a nice time. It eventually turns into a Dirty Martini and you find yourself dancing on the table with someone else's husband. The alcohol bully will eat away at your self-respect and defeat you every time.

Gambling

The gambling bully may be personified as a slot machine that says, "Come over here darling, pull my arm and you will see three gold bars that light up with bells ringing, telling you that you won." She will promise you a reward, but instead, she takes you down the path to financial ruin. The gambling bully will continue to say, "Come on, put in another quarter and another. You'll win this time." But guess what? Sadly, the odds are always in favor of the house.

Drugs

According to the National Center for Drug Abuse Statistics, in 2021 almost 32 million people, or 11.7% of the population were actively abusing drugs (including prescription drugs). The drug bully could be personified as a line of cocaine sitting on your counter acting as a lover calling your name by enticing you and begging you to take it. It's like a manipulation that is bullying and seducing you. It's calling you in a disguise on the surface and acts as your friend, but it ends up being a bully, knocks you down, and ruins your life.

Food

According to estimates by David Kessler, professor at UCSF and former commissioner of the FDA, there are more than 70 million food-addicted adults in the United States. This person will eat more than necessary for healthy living and proper nutrition. The food bully could be personified as a piece of chocolate cake saying, "Come over here and eat me. I taste so good." But instead of eating one piece, the food-addicted adult will end up eating the whole cake. Even though it satisfies your cravings and gives you instant gratification, it's short-lived. The chocolate cake may express itself initially as love and satisfaction but will only lead you to feel disgusted with yourself, depressed and guilty afterward. The continued abuse of food will lead to negative physical, emotional and social consequences such as obesity, heart disease, depression, low self-worth, and isolation.

Shopping
The shopping bully may not even be about the clothes but about short-term fulfillment that never really gives you any self-confidence, and once the item is worn, it just ends up sitting in your closet. The shopping bully could be personified as a Hermes bag using its voice, much like a Greek siren calling the sailors to the rocky shores and, unbeknownst to them, to their early deaths. If you have a shopping bully, it may lead to the death of your finances.

Sex
A sex bully could be personified as a billboard or advertisement in a magazine with a voice telling you that your worth is determined by how men value you. Maybe it's the Snapchat or Instagram app saying, "Come on, post another sexy photo. I promise more men will like you and follow you." You may think, "If I am sexy, then I have value and worth and more people will like me." Unfortunately, women and their bodies have become commodities. If we don't measure up to what culture or the marketing is saying, it negatively affects our emotions and feelings about ourselves.

How Can You Overcome Addiction Bullies?

Many people live with addiction bullies, and although they can wreak havoc on your life and your confidence, it is possible to recover. However, you will likely need the professional help of a medical doctor or psychologist and a strong support system to help you defeat these bullies.

Did You Identify Your Bully?

Identifying your bully and understanding how it impacts you is critical to your healing process. Your bully is a master at taking away your power and confidence. Once you give your power to your bully—your bully wins. Do you want Imposter Syndrome, alcohol or that nasty boss to control your life? If you want to be in control of your life and have more self-confidence, so you can be more fulfilled and achieve your goals, the information in this book can show you how. You'll learn to take your power back as you slowly start to defeat your bully while you work through the 5 Steps. Then, after you do the hard work, you can become more powerful and confident as your bully becomes powerless. Let's get started!

Self-doubt silences your spirit, but don't settle for giving it the last word.
TREVA GRAVES

CHAPTER Two
Self-Doubt

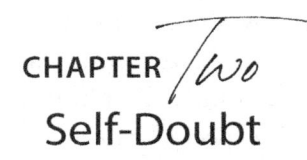

Self-doubt is uncertainty or anxiety about oneself and a lack of confidence in oneself and one's abilities.

It may seem surprising to the people in my life today that I grew up feeling so insecure and full of self-doubt. I felt I could never live up to the expectations of the people around me. Self-doubt was always inside of me, even before the bullying began. I hated this crippling feeling that grew stronger every day. I wanted more than anything to change that feeling, but I just didn't know how to do it.

I was raised by loving and supportive parents. They tucked me into bed every night with a kiss on my cheek. My father worked a blue-collar job, and my mother worked in retail. We were just a typical family living in the Midwest. My parents attended all my activities and sporting events. My father was my basketball, softball and volleyball coach throughout childhood. My mother taught me about beauty and fashion, which became my passion at an early age. She wanted me to look and feel beautiful every day. I think this was her way of trying to help me feel good about myself.

I was a good student, stayed out of trouble and obeyed my teachers. Despite all of this, I never felt like I fit in with girls in my classes, didn't have many friends and was severely bullied at school.

At the time, I couldn't understand why I felt so insecure, full of self-doubt and was the target of bullies.

Today, as a confident woman who has done the hard work to gain self-awareness and learn how to heal, I can look back at my childhood and understand some reasons for my insecurities and self-doubt.

Although I always felt safe and loved at home, no matter what was going on, it was hard to talk to my mother. She could be intimidating and was the authoritarian in our home and a perfectionist. Thankfully, my father was more laid back. My mother expected things to always be in order. Everything had its place. Our house was always clean, and you would never see dirty dishes in the sink. Pillows were fluffed on the couches and chairs, and my bedroom was always expected to be picked up and clean. I never left the house with an unmade bed. EVER! I remember one time in high school I threw a party for a few friends when my parents were out of town. When they returned home, my mom noticed a leaf had fallen off one of her plants and that's how she knew I had a party!

As a child, my mother loved me in a way where she attached her emotions to mine. She felt what I felt. If I was unhappy, she was unhappy. I suppose this is true for most mothers, but having a perfectionist mother caused me to experience a deep level of stress and anxiety trying to measure up to her expectations. I didn't want to let her down, knowing how deeply it would affect her. Of all the things in the world, the most important things my mother wanted for me was to be beautiful and happy. At the time, I felt neither of those things, although I tried so hard to make her happy. Don't get me wrong—I love my mother dearly, but living like that paralyzed me. I realize now that she was doing her best to help me. It was her way of showing she cared for and loved me.

My mother is tall and slender, with beautiful blue eyes and coal-black hair piled high on her head. I always teased her she needed a new "do," because she's had the same hairstyle since I was born! Wherever my mom went, people noticed her. She knew how to

CHAPTER TWO SELF-DOUBT

command a room and walked quickly with purpose and flair. She was super organized and always beautifully dressed. She modeled and was even a contestant in the Mrs. South Dakota America pageant!

My mother was an award-winning personal stylist at Macy's in the '80s. I was incredibly fortunate to have access to beautiful clothes, eye-catching shoes and handbags because of her employee discount. Although it was not typical for a young pre-teen or teen to wear Gloria Vanderbilt, Calvin Klein, Liz Claiborne, and Oscar de la Renta, I felt more comfortable all dressed up. It felt natural for me to be in beautiful clothes because that's all I really had, but it also became the reason I was bullied so much. My closet was every girl's dream, and my classmates were jealous of it.

I may have appeared superficial, but clothes became my "confidence suit of armor" because they hid how I felt inside. At least I thought they did. The beautiful clothes I had in my closet and wore daily made me feel better about myself. Whenever I wasn't dressed that way, I felt invisible. I desperately wanted to be noticed and accepted, but how I felt inside didn't match how I looked on the outside. When I entered junior high, I was hoping for a change for the better.

A new school, new people, new books, new teachers—a fresh start. Unfortunately, it didn't go as planned. I became the target of bullying by a group of "mean girls." My parents probably didn't know how much of a struggle it was for me to fit in. I sensed my parents suspected I was having difficulties, but I never, ever alluded to how bad it actually was because I didn't want to let them down. I wanted them to think everything was okay. I especially didn't want to let my mother down. I knew that it would have emotionally devastated her to know that I was feeling so low and hurting inside.

During junior high, there was one day that ultimately shaped the rest of my life. I am going to take you back to my darkest day. I woke up on a cloudy February day in 1980, and I knew this was the day I had been dreading. All the taunting, name-calling, prank phone calls at all hours of the day and night and cornering me in the bathroom not letting me out, was exhausting and terrifying. I was threatened for weeks that I would be beaten up so my face would never look the same again. I was living my life in fear. I was thrown into lockers and tripped as I walked down the hall to my next class, only to have my books fly all over the hallway. Students laughed at and ridiculed me. I was even kicked and thrown down a flight of 30 stairs and left there crying and bruised. And if you can believe it, all of this was done by girl bullies or "mean girls."

    I was mentally and emotionally sick to my stomach every single school day of my junior high years, just wanting the 3:30 p.m. bell to ring so I could go home and feel safe. But when mean girls Sheri, Lisa and Brenda came into my life, it progressively got worse. No wonder I weighed only 85 pounds at 15 years old. As I walked out of Axtell Park Junior High School in Sioux Falls, South Dakota, I could feel Sheri's breath on my neck. She was the "queen bee" of the group. The air was cold and heavy, and I knew they were coming for me.

    I crossed the street off the school grounds and walked onto the sidewalk near a snowbank. There was a group of kids following me, along with Sheri and her friends. I stopped, turned around to look at them and asked them to stop following me. Sheri pushed me into the snowbank and was yelling obscenities at me, telling me I was ugly, a slut, a whore, and a bitch. She called me prissy and said I was worthless, a "miss goody two shoes," and that no one liked me.

    I thought, "How could I be any of these things she was saying? I've never even had a boyfriend." I got up and told her to leave me alone. But she came at me again and slugged me across the face. I could feel her knuckles hit my cheekbone and instantly knew I would have a big, ugly bruise. I lunged back at her, trying to protect myself, but it was a lost cause. She pushed me to the ground again. The kids were all yelling and screaming, telling her to beat me up and taunting me with their cruel words. Before I knew it, she was sitting on my back, pulling my hair out and smacking me with her fists. The other two girls were hitting my head, stepping

CHAPTER TWO SELF-DOUBT

on me, and kicking my legs. I started crying and begged them to stop. I began yelling for someone to help me, but no one did.

Sheri turned me over and started smacking me in the face again. I put my hands up across my face to protect myself. She pulled chunks of hair from my head, and my lips started bleeding. I was begging them to stop. Some kids left, probably scared seeing me bleeding and crying. This attack felt like it went on forever. The punching, kicking in the ribs and smacking my face over and over was terrifying. Finally, I just stopped fighting back. In my mind, I couldn't believe this was happening to me. I wanted it to end. I felt myself go limp. I told myself just let them finish so they would leave me alone. Then everything went black.

I must have passed out for a few moments. I couldn't see, but I could hear voices around me. I felt like I was having an out-of-body experience. Finally, when Sheri and the girls realized I wasn't fighting anymore, they stepped back, looked down at me, and called me a "bitch" again and a host of other names. Sheri said that I deserved to be beaten up, and then they all walked away. The crowd started to disperse. Lying there in the snowbank, I felt my blood run down my face and turned to watch the formerly white, dirty snow turn red. That's how I felt—dirty. I thought to myself, "How could this happen? Why me? What did I ever do to them?" I really didn't understand why they chose to bully me.

It felt like hours passed as I tried to understand and digest the full brunt of what had happened, but it was only a few minutes. I was confused that no one came to assist me. No one stood up for me. Even as I continued to lie there, no one approached me. I'm sure the students were scared to help for fear of retaliation from Sheri and the other girl bullies. That's how much power she had. At that moment, I knew I was at the lowest point of my life. I was only 15 years old. To this day, that moment is still the lowest feeling I have ever experienced.

However, two things happened as I laid there. First, I decided I couldn't live my life in fear anymore, and I needed to make a change in my life. It had to start with me. I knew I never wanted to feel this way again. Second, I realized I was allowing this to happen because I never stood up for myself. I loathed myself and felt pathetic. As I had this thought, I looked up into the sky and studied the clouds. I noticed the clouds were parting, and the sun was trying to peek out. I pretended in my mind that God was listening and was trying to tell me something. I asked God to help me and prayed out loud to Him.

I thought that ray of sunshine on my bruised body and bloodied face was my sign. I was looking for anyone or anything to help me. Right then, I made a choice that I was going to change my life for good. I was leaving the weak, insecure me behind, and the new me was going to emerge. I didn't know how to do it, but I knew I needed help. I was tired of feeling worthless and insecure. I was tired of waking up in a pit of pity and self-doubt. For four years, girls and boys had been picking on me and beating me up.

It was so shocking to me that *girls* were beating me up. I mean, what kind of girl would do this? All I wanted was to have friends and fit in like everyone else. In those days, "bullying" wasn't even a word that was used. Being bullied was a horrific experience that ultimately shaped the course of my life. I was through feeling defeated. It was time to find the courage to be brave and work on myself. I needed a fresh start and a new perspective. I needed help to become self-confident.

As I continued to lay there, I created another world in my brain where I saw myself as liked, popular and successful. I disassociated myself from the horrible situation I was in. I wanted to live in that imaginary world, not my real world. I also wanted desperately to be loved and accepted. I knew my family loved me, but I wanted to be loved by others. I knew I could become the person I wanted to be. I was a good person and kind to people. That was a good start, but I also knew I had a lot of work to do.

I finally got myself up out of the snowbank and walked home. I was bruised, bloodied and hurt everywhere. I felt like I had been

CHAPTER TWO SELF-DOUBT

hit by a truck. I don't think I even realized how badly I was beaten until I got home, took off my clothes and looked in the mirror. When my parents saw me, they were horrified and immediately wanted to know everything. I told them about the attack. My parents were devastated to see me like that. They called the school and the girls' parents, which led to several meetings.

The school officials had never seen an incident like this in all their years in education. The girl bullies were held accountable by the school officials. I was advised to file charges with the police department, but I didn't. When I think back on it, I should have. I finished the school year without ever hearing another word from the girl bullies.

After the bullying incident, my parents transferred me to the Catholic high school in town. My favorite part of attending a parochial school was that I wore a uniform every day. For most kids, wearing a uniform was awful, but I didn't mind it at all. Everyone looked the same, and that was okay with me because it made me feel like I fit in. Changing schools also gave me a fresh start with new people so I could make new friends. I loved being there and felt a sense of community in a smaller school where I could practice my faith. I thought to myself that things were only going to get better. At least, I prayed they would.

"Self-confidence can be learned, practiced, and mastered—just like any other skill. Once you master it, everything in your life will change for the better."
BARRIE DAVENPORT

ACTIVITY #1 – LOOK FOR THEMES

In this exercise, I want you to think about what causes you to feel insecure. What are your automatic negative thoughts? Do you notice any themes? When I did this exercise, I noticed common themes.

See if what you noted matches up with the list below. Check whether any of these beliefs feel correct to you, even if you understand that they are unrealistic.

- ☐ I'm not good enough.
- ☐ I can't do anything right.
- ☐ I'm worthless.
- ☐ I'm a failure.
- ☐ I'm abnormal.
- ☐ I'm not wanted.
- ☐ I'm unlovable.
- ☐ I don't fit in.
- ☐ I'm all alone.
- ☐ I'm not important.
- ☐ I'm not as good as other people.
- ☐ I'm sure to be rejected.
- ☐ I am weak.
- ☐ I don't measure up to others.
- ☐ I am unsuccessful.
- ☐ I can't handle anything.
- ☐ I'm a loser.
- ☐ I have to be perfect.
- ☐ My needs don't matter.
- ☐ I'm not a worthwhile person.

To develop a better sense of self, you need to own your values and goals. This goes a long way toward developing a healthy sense of self.

- *Try setting some boundaries.* Say "no" to the things that have nothing to do with what you love or value.

CHAPTER TWO SELF-DOUBT

- *Get comfortable with being alone.* It's okay to go to a movie by yourself!

- *Avoid comparing yourself to others.* Catch yourself when you feel like you don't measure up to another person. We are all on different paths in life.

- *Know what motivates you.* Structure your life around what makes you stick with a goal—not what works for a friend.

- *Be a rebel.* If you feel like everyone is doing something that doesn't match up with what you believe or care about, be brave enough to go another way.

ACTIVITY #2 – SELF-DOUBT QUIZ

Self-doubt is crippling and will put limits on what you can achieve in your life. Take this short quiz and give yourself 10 points for every answer of "true."

---

1. I don't speak up and share my thoughts and opinions in a group or meeting. _____

2. I am often afraid of making mistakes. _____

3. I often believe that I am not good enough. _____

4. I am afraid to go outside of my comfort zone. _____

5. I believe that others will not like me. _____

6. I replay conversations and think of things I could have said better. _____

7. I do not like to try new things. _____

8. I worry about what others think of me. _____

9. I believe I have failed many times. _____

10. I often think negative, catastrophic thoughts that start with, "What if…" _____

0-40	You are doing fantastic work on treating yourself kindly.
40-60	You struggle to feel worthy, but other times you are comfortable with yourself.
60-80	You often hold back from living fully because of fears and insecurity.
80-100	You are struggling with insecurity and believing in yourself.

No matter your score, this book can help you start your journey to living free of fear and guide you to take small steps each day to feel self-confident.

To begin your self-doubt detox to defeat insecurity and start believing in yourself, I'm going to share with you how I began to build confidence. Confidence is a gift you give yourself and starts with giving yourself permission to be you. You will make some mistakes along the way, and it might be a rocky road for a while. But that's okay. Rome wasn't built in a day, and neither is confidence. It's a journey you'll be on for the rest of your life. I still have moments of self-doubt, but I always go back to what I learned and have developed a framework for you to start building yours.

The BLOOM Methodology stands for BELIEVE, LOVE, OBSERVE, OPPORTUNITY, and MENTOR. This is the framework that I'll share with you to help you detox entirely from your self-doubt and feel confident and worthy every day. You must believe you deserve to live a BOLD, BRAVE and BRILLIANT life.

CHAPTER TWO SELF-DOUBT

Now, before we start to BLOOM, I want you to do this—I want you to affirm your value. It's helpful to have a notebook or journal, take inventory and write down everything you are doing right. Take stock of all your accomplishments. Daily, I want you to write down every little thing, from making your bed and brushing your teeth, to finishing up a project at work. Everything counts, and this will help you start taking "micro-movements" or baby steps in building your self-confidence. I refer to my list when I am having a weak moment. Our brains have neuroplasticity, which means we can re-train our nerves to think positive rather than negative. Physio-pedia.com defines it as: "the ability of the nervous system to change its activity in response to intrinsic or extrinsic stimuli by reorganizing its structure, functions, or connections." Isn't that amazing?

Micro-movements will give you a sense of accomplishment every day, provide you with purpose and help you move out of insecure feelings you may be experiencing. This activity is something I strongly believe in and is a great starting point to change your life. Let this become a routine for you.

Once you begin seeing things on paper that you're completing and doing every day, your self-doubt will begin to fade. You will see your accomplishments! A change in your mindset from negative to positive will form as this is needed to start believing in yourself. Remember this, because positive change begins with YOU, and it happens NOW. Whether you have others in your life who believe in you or not, their belief, or lack of, will never change YOUR belief.

Journaling is a great mindfulness exercise to identify your thoughts and become aware of patterns. I used to think journaling was silly. Now, I've realized the positive impact it has on my attitude and beliefs. You can even find that writing down your worries leads to solutions and possibilities that come to you as you write. Every day, set an intention and write about what you feel and how it affects your day. Then, reflect and be honest with yourself, giving yourself a chance to delve deeply.

DEVELOP INTENTION

Identify Your Thought Patterns

Today, I am constantly thinking about _____

It makes me feel _____

Instead, I would like to feel _____

Practicing Mindfulness

I can't stop thinking about _____

It makes me worry about _____

I can look at the problem from another angle _____

Gratitude

Today, I am grateful for _____

I feel lucky because _____

I appreciate _____

Accomplishments

When I have a more positive mindset, my life is _____

Today, I accomplished _____

When I am positive, I get excited about _____

Great work!

    You are on your way to the first step in BLOOM. Now it's time to start BELIEVING in YOURSELF!

Believe in yourself. No one else can do this for you.
TREVA GRAVES

CHAPTER *Three*
Believe

Step 1 to Beat Your Bully and Bloom Confidence

To believe means to accept something as true.

After the horrible bullying incident, my mother enrolled me in the Bernice Johnson School of Modeling in Sioux Falls, South Dakota, to help me build my confidence. I don't think she ever intended for me to become a professional model. She just wanted to help me feel better about myself and build self-confidence. I had zero confidence when I walked in the door on my first day of modeling school. I was shy, nervous and had no idea what to expect.

Bernice Johnson, who was a gorgeous, tall, blonde older woman, greeted me. The first thing she said to me in the sweetest voice I ever heard was that I looked beautiful. She probably said that to every girl who walked in, but I didn't care. It was the way she said it and how it made me feel that put a smile on my face—even though inside, I felt like crawling into a hole. I was immediately fascinated by what I saw at the modeling school. In my daydreams, I could see myself on a stage, being a model and maybe even taking part in a pageant someday. I looked around the room and was intrigued by everything. I thought, "Could I *really* be like one of the girls and women in pictures, magazines and posters that were displayed on the walls?"

I had always been skinny and my track coach in junior high said that I could, "Run like the wind." It reminded me of the Christopher Cross song, "Ride Like the Wind," which was one of my favorites (I actually got to meet him as he was my music teacher's nephew). But as I entered high school, I was going through a growth spurt and had put on a little weight. I would look in the mirror and think my face was so fat, and my tummy wasn't as flat as it used to be. I would get ready for every modeling session by putting on a nice dress or a blazer and pants with high-heeled shoes. I always showed up wearing beautiful clothes that made me feel good on the outside because I desperately wanted to make a good impression on Bernice. She was my instructor for a few sessions, and I enjoyed her, but things were about to change.

One day, Bernice introduced me to a new instructor she had recently hired. Her name was Janet May. I took one look at Janet and knew she wasn't from Sioux Falls. I could just tell by how she looked, talked and moved. She was sophisticated and refined. She was a tall, slender woman, "dressed to the nines" with long black hair and a smile that was warm and friendly. Janet taught me how to make a good first impression, communicate, walk, talk, sit, and have a stage presence.

We practiced posing, turning, walking, and even answering questions, interview style, so I could think quickly on my feet and with a microphone in my hand. Janet was my instructor, but also someone I could talk to about my deep insecurity of never feeling like I fit in. She became my coach, helping me build my confidence and teaching me strategies to start believing in myself. I listened carefully to every word she said. I wanted to emulate her as she was so comfortable just being herself. She was so graceful, and everything seemed to be so easy for her like it was second nature. I wanted to be like that. I knew if I worked hard enough, I could.

CHAPTER THREE BELIEVE

As I finished up my last sessions at the modeling school, I remembered lying in that snowbank one year earlier, reliving that horrible day but also knowing I had changed. I still had so much to learn. I was on my way to building confidence and self-esteem. The awful feeling of being bullied, scared and insecure had become too much to bear. As I worked with Janet, I began to let go of those feelings. She taught me to look ahead because I couldn't change the past—but I *could* control my future. Slowly, I started to allow myself to do this and felt myself believe in the change I was feeling—the feeling of being uniquely me. I am so thankful that Janet came into my life when I needed her. She was not only my modeling instructor but my supporter, teacher and friend.

> *"You've always had the power, my dear, you just had to learn it for yourself."*
>
> **GLINDA, THE GOOD WITCH OF THE NORTH, WIZARD OF OZ**

According to the American Confidence Institute, boys lose 30% of their confidence, and girls lose 50% by the time they are 16 years old. Those figures are so disappointing, but unfortunately, true. How can we encourage and facilitate confidence at a much earlier age? I believe it begins in our homes and at school.

As I got older and graduated from college, I started my career as a business professional in the banking and insurance industry. I remember wearing power suits in the '80s. Big hair, big jewelry, big shoulder pads, heavy makeup, nylons and pumps were the "uniform" of fashion. It gave me a sense of power to wear those clothes! I was still working on being "me," and I was making progress. One day, in my early 20s, I ran into a guy from high school, and he said, "You really blossomed after high school." I guess you could say, I was a late bloomer!

I was a model for over 25 years and loved doing everything from hand, print and runway modeling to commercial acting. I worked and modeled for Macy's during my late teens and 20s and even into my 40s. I was on numerous local and national commercials for car dealerships, retail and drug stores, hotels, and many others. I became a makeup artist, first for Clinique and then modeled for Lancôme and Estee Lauder. I love makeup and think I've tried nearly every product ever made! I discovered I was very good as a makeup artist. I became a certified makeup artist and have applied makeup to hundreds of faces over the years.

Later, I eventually followed in my mother's footsteps and worked in retail, started a business and became a personal stylist, doing many of the same things my mother did. I've worked with hundreds of women building their image and style and now their personal brands. It's been an honor and such a rewarding experience. They've let me into their personal lives, and we have shared many stories with each other. I've learned that I am not alone in how I have felt. I hope they've learned from me as much as I've learned from them. Feeling good in clothes, as I have experienced, can have a profound effect on how you feel. There is even research to back it up!

I also help women feel good about the way they look by gaining body confidence. Body confidence is the ability to feel completely at home in your body, no matter the size or shape. It's essentially challenging yourself to accept and eventually love who you are today, just as you are, instead of the visceral need for "perfection." The underlying theme with many of my clients is the belief that if they are thin and beautiful, then they will be happy. I have helped them understand that this is not true. *Feeling* beautiful is more important than physically looking that way. Having body acceptance and loving yourself are key components to living a happy and healthy life.

Growing up and into my 20s, I felt the need to be as "perfect" as I could be to have people think I was confident. In the end, it made me miserable. There was no way I could maintain or achieve that. Once I started just accepting myself for who I was and what I looked like, I felt the need to be perfect subside. I still like to look my absolute best, but the body I have today is very different from the body I had in my 20s. Getting older and going through menopause changes a woman in more ways than one. It's essential to allow yourself to embrace your changes because if you strive for perfection, you will never be satisfied. That is simply an unhealthy way to live.

> *"People often say that beauty is in the eye of the beholder. I say that the most liberating thing about beauty is realizing that you are the beholder."*
> **SALMA HAYEK**

Loving your own body, as obvious as the notion may seem, is often easier said than done. It's startling that 70% of women between the ages of 18-30 dislike their bodies. Men aren't much better off as, 45% say they are dissatisfied with their bodies too. If you find yourself feeling low about your own body, you're not alone. Changing the way you think requires daily effort. When was the last time you gave your body a gift just to say, "Hey, thanks for sticking with me"? Carve out some time to lie in the grass, take a bubble bath or walk up the hill to a pretty view. A good nap can be a gift, too.

The world is full of negative messages about bodies. Balance that negative noise with some good, positive perspectives. Look for positive people who practice self-love and who will also encourage you to be who you are. I have cleared my social media feed of people trying to be someone they're not. Every time a negative thought about your body pops into your mind, counter it with something positive. Treat your body with the same kindness you'd treat a friend. If you're about to say something you'd feel bad saying about a friend's body, then don't say it!

People come in all shapes and sizes. One person is beautiful in one way and the next person in some other way. And isn't that how it should be? Imagine how boring it would be if there were only one way to be and to feel beautiful. Comparing yourself to others can leave you feeling like you don't look the way you should, but you're not supposed to look like someone else. You are supposed to look like you!

What works for me is to think healthy, not skinny. Exercise and a healthy diet aren't punishment. This is one way we show respect and appreciation for our bodies. Honor your body with nourishing meals and exercises that you ENJOY. I love taking 30-minute daily walks. Walking or taking a bike ride not only clears my head, but it's good for my body. Believe that a healthy mindset will lead you to a healthy life. Believe that you are more than just the way you look and feel great about who you are.

"Believe" is such a powerful word. I remember lying in the snowbank, looking at that ray of sunshine poking through the clouds, giving me a glimmer of hope that someone was listening to me. That's when I decided to start believing I could make a positive change in myself. I knew it started with me, and it was a choice I needed to make to begin living a life free of fear and self-doubt. Janet taught me through my modeling sessions that I needed to believe in myself—and I was going to live that belief. It was making a major shift in my mindset that helped me get started. I was going to start taking my power back.

Being certain about your values, thoughts and purpose breeds confidence! The movie "Rocky," starring Sylvester Stallone, was such a powerful movie as it had so many life lessons. I watch it from time to time to remind myself of the struggles he had to overcome. Watch it sometime for a little inspiration. Remember the picture of Rocky running up the steps of the Philadelphia Museum

CHAPTER THREE BELIEVE

of Art, jumping up and down with his hands in the air? That was such a poignant moment!

> *"Until you start believing in yourself, you ain't gonna have a life."*
> **ROCKY BALBOA**

When I was bullied, I made the mistake of giving my power to the bully. When you start to believe in yourself, you begin to cultivate your confidence. Pretty soon, I saw myself standing on those steps, jumping up and down. As soon as my belief system started to change, I took my power back. I saw myself becoming Rocky and began the process of defeating one of my bullies.

We've all made mistakes and been stuck in our pity pits, but growth can happen by changing your mindset with the method I'm giving you now. The growth is in the BLOOM Method, which is why I believe that positive self-talk is so essential. I can't stress this enough. Digging deep within yourself and discovering what has been holding you back is the key to moving into where you want to be.

I begin each day by saying a positive affirmation and setting a goal for myself. Sometimes my goal is to try not to have a negative thought, and sometimes, it's about crossing items off my daily list of tasks I need to accomplish. I'm old school, and I still like paper planners, reading the actual newspaper and making lists on post-its!

There are many benefits to believing in yourself. Think about people in your life or at work who strongly believe in their abilities and themselves. You'll note that they seem to accomplish a lot daily. They have tons of energy and are always completing their to-do list. They are just nice people less likely to judge others and much more likely to encourage them instead. Wouldn't it be wonderful to truly believe in yourself and be that person you admire?

SEVEN WAYS TO BELIEVE IN YOURSELF

1. Be realistic about your goals

Accomplishing goals makes us feel good about ourselves. Setting goals that are achievable on a daily and weekly basis sets us on the path toward success and the belief that we can accomplish great things. I set goals for myself every day.

2. Surround yourself with positivity

When you keep the company of those who bring you down, you won't feel good about yourself. Surround yourself with positive and generally happy people. Rid yourself of as much negativity as possible. Lose those friends who never have a positive thing to say.

3. Acknowledge accomplishments and passions

As you accomplish something, no matter how trivial, first acknowledge that you have completed something. All your simple accomplishments are significant for your self-esteem. Keep writing them down daily. It's the micro-movements that count! Think about and acknowledge what you enjoy doing by pursuing your passions as often as possible.

4. Share what you have to offer

Are you an expert at something? Most of us have at least one thing we are passionate about and excel at. Share your expertise with someone else. Helping others learn something new strengthens our belief in ourselves. Share your unique ingredient and exploit your uniqueness in the service of others. Wouldn't it be amazing if we all shared our unique talents with the world? It's why you are here on earth!

CHAPTER THREE BELIEVE

5. Reach for the stars

As cliché as it may sound, go for that job you think may be out of reach or learn that skill you have been putting off because it seems much too difficult. Even if you don't succeed in reaching the furthest star, you're certain to capture something extremely rewarding on the way down from all that effort. I would rather try something and fail than not try it at all. I've had my share of failures, but I choose to live with no regrets.

6. Don't be afraid to speak up

If you have a question or need clarification, speak up. If you see another way a process within your office can work more efficiently, tell someone. Don't be afraid to use your voice and share your thoughts and ideas. The more you do it, the more comfortable you become. I used to be that wallflower who never said anything in a meeting or a group. Not anymore! It will build your confidence.

7. Take care of yourself—You're important!

This one is so important because you are. Believing in yourself comes down to you and your journey through life on your terms. Set boundaries you are comfortable with, take care of your body, continue to learn, and surround yourself with family and friends that love and support you no matter what.

POSITIVE AFFIRMATIONS

To bust out of the pity party you may be throwing for yourself, you need to believe in yourself daily. My new mantra became, "If you can believe it, you can achieve it!" "B" in the BLOOM Framework is for BELIEVE. Get up each day, look in the mirror, say three positive affirmations, and believe in your words. I completely believe in the power of positive self-talk. It's been part of my morning routine for 40 years. Some people may not want to use positive affirmations as they feel a little silly saying them out loud in front of the bathroom mirror, but remember, successful people do what others don't. Positive self-talk can change how you feel. It's based upon emotion, and it can give you the power to cause a physiological change in the way you are feeling.

When you have a negative thought, it's important to acknowledge it and find a way to put it out of your mind or "cancel" it. That's where the power of positive self-talk comes in. Here is a little framework I use if I feel a negative thought or an imposter bully talking to me. I call it "ACT."

ACT means to acknowledge, cancel and transform.

A – Acknowledge the thought.

C – Cancel the thought.

T – Transform your thoughts into a new, positive one.

If you tend to have a negative outlook on things, don't expect to become a positive person overnight. With practice, your self-talk will contain less negativity and you will have more self-acceptance. You may even become less critical of others and the world around you. There are so many benefits of positive thinking. When you decide to ACT and think positively about yourself, you may even be better able to handle everyday stress more constructively. This has certainly been the case for me.

To begin using positive self-talk, start by following one simple rule. Don't say anything to yourself that you wouldn't say to anyone else. Be gentle and encouraging with yourself. ACT will help you master this. If a negative thought enters your mind—and it will—acknowledge and evaluate it rationally, cancel it and transform it by saying a positive affirmation about yourself. It may help to think about things that you have gratitude for.

Here are some examples of ACT:

CHAPTER THREE BELIEVE

Negative Self Talk	**Positive Thinking**
There is no way it will work.	I can try to make it work.
It's too complicated.	I'll tackle this from a different angle.
I've never done this before.	It's an opportunity to learn something new.
I'm not going to get any better at this.	I'll give it another try.
No one bothers to communicate with me.	I will try to start the conversation.

Changing your mindset takes work and intention. Try listening to an empowering podcast or re-adopt a hobby you enjoyed in the past. Journaling and keeping a list of things you are grateful for can also help support your transformation. But you must start speaking to yourself in a positive way to break the pattern of negative self-talk.

One strategy that works for me is having a morning routine. It can have a significant impact on your mindset throughout the day. For example, after I get dressed in something that makes me feel confident and say my positive affirmations, I sometimes do a quick 3-minute meditation to prepare myself for the day. I also make sure I nourish myself by getting enough sleep and eating a healthy diet.

Your mindset impacts how you see the world and how you feel. As I mentioned, it takes intentional effort, but the payoff is well worth it. Everyone's version of success is unique. We all have our own goals that align with our values and vision for our lives. Whatever goals you have, to achieve them, you need a positive mindset. I hope ACT can help you get started!

Here is one affirmation to inspire you. This is the first affirmation I ever said to myself, and I continue to say it to this day!

"I am valuable, I am capable and I am worth it!"

Go ahead and say it. I promise you will feel better once you start saying positive affirmations to yourself every day. If you want a list to help get you started, you can download a free copy of my "100 Positive Daily Affirmations to Believe in YOU" at www.bloompersonalbranding.com/resources.

ACTIVITY #3 – SELF-ASSESSMENT: ACCEPT AND BELIEVE IN YOUR STRENGTHS

If you've ever battled low self-confidence and lack of belief in yourself, it may come from resisting compliments and good fortune. Women are particularly more averse than men to acknowledging their strengths, believing they will be seen as bragging or egotistical. Accepting your strengths isn't about building yourself up or comparison to others. You don't need to tell yourself you are the best salesperson, parent or cook. When you've worked hard, give yourself credit! When you do a good job or try something new, let yourself feel some pride.

Accepting your strengths helps you believe in yourself and keeps your weaknesses in perspective, which is one of the keys to walking through the world with confidence. As humans, we are all flawed and imperfect. Accepting this belief is a critical component of understanding and practicing self-compassion and believing in ourselves. It requires genuine kindness, acceptance, grace and compassion toward our flaws, not just awareness.

CHAPTER THREE BELIEVE

Identify Strengths

Make a list of your strengths and be proud of them.

Compliments I have received _____

Challenges I've overcome _____

An important role I've fulfilled _____

An important task I've tackled _____

Skills I enjoy using regardless of the task _____

A time I've helped someone else _____

When you are finished, read over what you have written. Are there any themes?

List three or more of your strengths below:

_____

_____

_____

Remember, confidence isn't the same as arrogance. It's the knowledge that you can continue to act in line with your values, no matter what life throws at you.

ACTIVITY #4 – FIVE-MINUTE CONFIDENCE

A commitment I made to myself was that I would start and end every day with positive thoughts. I know we all can take five minutes of our day to focus on believing in ourselves.

Here is a little framework to help you get started.

In the morning, go to your closet and put on something that makes you feel fabulous.

1. Wearing clothes we feel good in builds the feeling of self-confidence.

2. Next, go to the mirror and say three positive affirmations.

3. At the end of the day, take out your journal and write down three good things that happened during the day. It can be anything positive, big or small!

Always start and end your day on a positive note!

Now that you have learned to believe in yourself, let's talk about loving yourself.

*Loving yourself means choosing
to love yourself first.*
TREVA GRAVES

CHAPTER Four
Love Yourself

Step 2 to Beat Your Bully and Bloom Confidence

Self-Love is having regard for one's well-being and happiness.

After being rejected by my classmates, growing up and into my teens, I developed a need to be loved and accepted. My family loved and accepted me, but I desperately wanted to feel love from a boyfriend because I thought it would validate me. I didn't date a lot in high school, but my social life changed when I got to college. I joined a sorority and became involved with parties, drinking and staying up late at night. It was fun for a while, but that lifestyle became exhausting. Suddenly, I had guys calling me all the time; I went on a lot of dates and had boyfriends. I felt I was finally getting the attention I wanted. I had been the "wallflower" or the odd one out most of my life, and when I started getting a lot of attention, it felt amazing and gave me a false sense of confidence.

Getting caught up in all the attention, I started to engage in promiscuous behavior. It was unhealthy to think that having sex meant someone loved and cared about me. I didn't find the love I was searching for, and I realized I was not only hurting myself, but I hurt others, too. My behavior negatively affected some of my female relationships. This was another time when I had to step back and take note of what I was doing. I needed to make a change. Once I stopped the promiscuous behavior and started to focus on myself—my values, goals and dreams—I realized what bad decisions I was making and vowed not to do that again. But I soon experienced another setback.

While in college, I met and fell for a guy who was not right for me. We dated off and on, but I still went back to him after our fights and disagreements. He was very possessive and always wanted to know where I was and with whom. He would get angry so easily if he felt he didn't have control over our relationship. This was a warning sign for what was to come. If he became upset, he would express his anger physically to the point of grabbing my arms and would squeeze so tight that bruises formed. He would drink excessively, call me names and make threats against me if I told him I was going to leave him.

After several months of continued abuse, I finally had enough and left him. We broke up after a horrible physical altercation in a parking lot at a local college bar. I didn't see or hear from him for about a year. Then completely out of the blue, he called and said he wanted to see me as he had just received a terrible health diagnosis and needed some support. I could hear the fear in his voice. He said he just wanted someone to talk to, so I agreed to meet him.

While in college, he had been a pitcher for the University of South Dakota's baseball team, and he was really good. I enjoyed attending his games and tried to think about those good times as I drove to another town to visit him. I also thought about what he was about to tell me. As we sat in the living room of his parents' home, he shared the story of what happened.

He had dreamed of trying out for a major league baseball team, and it was about to come true. He was so excited as he had worked for this moment his entire life. However, the day before his trip, he woke up not feeling well and scheduled a quick appointment with his doctor. He was having some trouble breathing and thought it

CHAPTER FOUR LOVE YOURSELF

was just a viral infection or allergies. After some tests, the doctor shared the devastating news that my former boyfriend's lungs were full of cancer. He was completely shocked and knew that this was most likely the end of his lifelong dream. He immediately started treatment at the Mayo Clinic in Rochester, Minnesota.

We stayed in touch for months as he was receiving chemotherapy. His trips to and from Rochester were physically and emotionally draining. I didn't go on any of those trips as I was working, but I saw what was happening not only to his body but to his mind and well-being. It was an awful time to start a relationship again. He needed me so much, but I was very reluctant to get involved any more deeply than as friends. I knew I shouldn't let this happen. But I did. I had so many second thoughts and should have listened to my instincts. But I didn't. I put his needs ahead of mine and gave in to his pleas to stay with him. I felt so sorry for him. He promised me this time, things would be different. I eventually moved to be near him, and he asked me to marry him. At first, I didn't know what to say. I wasn't sure if I really loved him or just felt sorry for him. After a short courtship, we ended up getting married, but things went wrong almost immediately, and I knew I had made a terrible mistake.

Over time, as his health improved and he started feeling better, he went back to his old ways. He was so angry. Angry at life, at God, at everything. He would say things like, "Why did this happen to me?" "Why would God let this happen?" He started drinking to cover up the pain and frustration of losing his dream. Not surprisingly, he took that anger out on me.

After many nights of him drinking too much and not coming home, along with bouts of anger that he would take out on me, I decided to leave for good. As I packed my bags and headed for the door, he walked in drunk and saw what I was doing. I told him I was leaving him and that I could no longer live this way. He became enraged and lunged at me. I ran by him as quickly as I could out of our apartment. He chased me down the stairs into the parking lot while I juggled my bags and hanging clothes.

He caught up with me as I tried to get into my car. He threw me to the ground, and my bags and clothes were strewn over the pavement. As he sat on top of me, he began hitting me as I screamed for help. He continued to beat my face and turned me over so I was facing the ground. He began pounding my face onto the pavement. I felt my nose being crushed as I cried and screamed for help. I started having flashbacks of the "mean girls" beating me up years earlier.

Finally, some tenants in the apartment building came outside to help. As I yelled to call 911, my husband grabbed one of the hangers that fell to the ground, bent the curved hook straight and prepared to stab me. I put my arms up to protect myself while a man from the apartment building rushed to my side to help pull him off me. My husband took off running into the night. The police finally showed up, he was apprehended later and brought to the police station. It was another horrible experience. I thought, "How could I let this happen to me again?" I was angry and disgusted with myself. He eventually recovered and became cancer-free, but I was long gone before that day ever happened.

My husband was a bully, and I thank God I ended the marriage quickly. I was married for only six months. I was 22 years old and divorced. We married in the Catholic church, so I decided to have the marriage annulled and was thankful that the church granted my request. I was sad and embarrassed that I had ever let something like this happen to me. I realized I was trying to please everyone but myself. I didn't want to hurt him by leaving him even though he continually hurt me. I was still on my journey to self-confidence, and the mistake I made again? I gave my power away. I didn't stand up for myself until it was almost too late. I have no doubt that if I hadn't fought back at the last moment, he would have stabbed me.

No one deserves to be treated like this. If you are in a situation like this, leave immediately. No matter how often your spouse or significant other tells you they're going to change, don't believe it

CHAPTER FOUR LOVE YOURSELF

until they show you. They need time and professional help to work on themselves. You deserve better. ***If you find yourself in this situation, please refer to Chapter One, where I suggest a practical plan for getting out.***

Sometimes, confidence ebbs and flows in life. This was a time in my life when the "ebb" was real. I needed to detox my self-doubt and insecurities, regain my power, refocus on building a positive mindset, and start to heal once again. I needed to use the steps that eventually became BLOOM to help me get there.

About six months after my divorce, I started working in a law firm as a legal secretary. The firm was hiring a new attorney who was graduating from Creighton Law School in Omaha, Nebraska. The attorney I worked for went to school with the new lawyer, and they were in the same fraternity at the University of South Dakota. Since I attended the same college, I was curious to know who this new guy was. I was told that I might also do some administrative work for him.

When the new lawyer started, I never thought in my wildest dreams that I would go out with him. He was very nice, professional, clean-cut, and intelligent. He had his life in order, which was something I admired about him, as I was still a work in progress. If someone had told me I would marry him, I would have said they were crazy. After some time went by, my boss set us up on a date as he felt we might be a good match, and it turns out he was right!

He was more than a good match. He was a godsend for me because he gave me the love and acceptance I'd desired for so long. He was good to me, supported me and I was happy spending time with him. Even though it wasn't love at first sight, I thought he was handsome and just an overall wonderful human being. He wined and dined me, took me on vacations, and we spent all our time together. Our relationship grew over time, and I became the yin to his yang. We fell in love and dated for five years before we got married. We certainly had some differences in our backgrounds, but it still worked. Looking back on it, I'm glad it happened that way. He was responsible, dependable and consistent. He still is today.

Our relationship was something I had never experienced before, making it even more special. He loved me for me, the good and the bad, my successes and failures, all my imperfections. We've had our fair share of struggles, but I know he has my back, and I have his. Marriages experience highs and lows. I think if you can keep it "warm," that is, be consistent, supportive, respectful, and loving, then you can have a successful marriage.

Now, after all the mistakes I made and everything that has happened, you are probably wondering if I was ever in therapy, and the answer to that is a resounding yes! As I write this, I am thinking, "Was I *really* like that? I've come so far from this!" I am one of those people who enjoyed going to therapy sessions. They helped me see myself in a different light and forced me to dig deep into myself to discover the root cause of my issues. I also needed to learn how to love myself. Therapy helped me see some things about myself that I needed to work on and change, other than my confidence issues.

On my journey to self-confidence, I discovered that the practice of loving yourself plays a huge part in your self-esteem. It's something I incorporate into my life, and it helps me stay balanced and focused on what I want for myself. I've included some ways for you to understand what self-love is and some ways to start practicing self-love. These strategies have helped me.

Self-love is believing you are a valuable and worthy person. An example of self-love is when you have a positive view of yourself and are confident in yourself and your place in the world. Loving yourself is a crucial part of growing your self-confidence. I used to think that self-love sounded indulgent and luxurious. It goes well beyond a massage, a pedicure, a glass of wine, or soaking in the tub—although all those things sound wonderful! It involves so much more. It's about developing a deep honesty in ourselves to create an authentic life in which our choices and decisions nurture and reflect our true selves and values.

CHAPTER FOUR LOVE YOURSELF

Have you ever looked around at other successful women and thought, "How do they do it? How do they manage to feel so *good*?" I wanted so desperately to find out, so I could feel happy and well. During my childhood, I experienced such crippling low self-esteem and self-loathing that I didn't see a way out. That is until I started my modeling classes with Bernice and Janet. I explored the ideas and habits of self-love and self-care. I read books and magazines and watched how women carried and expressed themselves. I observed how they walked and talked. Now, remember this was the early 1980s, and self-love wasn't a term that was as popular as it is today. So, how does this relate to having confidence and self-worth? What I found out was that it mattered a lot!

Self-love is the fuel that allows you to reach your full potential and is filled with compassion, grace and gentleness. Making space and prioritizing ourselves allow us to embrace our lives completely and wholeheartedly. Self-love is learning to extend kindness toward ourselves, even when we struggle and suffer. It is extending forgiveness to ourselves when we make mistakes—and God knows I've made many. Self-love means prioritizing ourselves and giving ourselves permission to find and believe in our strengths and gifts, as I mentioned in the last chapter. Sometimes it means putting ourselves first, making space to identify our wants and needs and setting boundaries.

Self-love is not perfection, nor is it always being happy. It's not based on your achievements or external measurements of success—nor is it based on shame, criticism or fear. True self-love comes from within, even when you screw up or take a wrong turn in life. Practicing self-love is a choice. Choose to love yourself every day and add the "L," which is the next layer of the BLOOM Framework.

It's like living your life from the inside out, not the outside in. You must take care of your heart, your mind and your soul. It's your well-being, and I can tell you that when my well-being is off, I'm *really* off. We've probably all used the term, "I need a mental health day." What I'm saying is that we need a day for ourselves to re-group, take some time to relax, give our brains a break, and do something that makes our hearts happy.

SELF-AWARENESS + SELF-FORGIVENESS = SELF-ACCEPTANCE

12 SELF-LOVE IDEAS

Practicing self-love is vital for loving and accepting who we are so that we can be confident every day. I am sharing with you some ideas that I believe will help you in your daily life to love yourself more. I have practiced many of these things at different times in my life. They are simple, practical and multifaceted in their benefits.

1. Stop comparing yourself to others

We're socialized to be competitive, so comparing ourselves to others is natural. But it can be dangerous. There's just no point in comparing yourself to anyone else on the planet because there's only one of you. Instead, focus on yourself and your journey. The shift of energy alone will help you feel more free. I gave myself permission to be uniquely me, even though it took me years to feel comfortable in my skin. I gave myself the grace to learn at the pace that felt right for me. You can do it too!

2. Don't worry about other's opinions

In that same vein, don't worry about what family, friends or society thinks or expects of you. You can't make everyone happy, so it's a waste of time to try, and it will only slow you down on your journey to being the best you. When I was young and trying to fit in, I worried way too much about what other people thought of me. It's so freeing when you let this go. Our world today is much more open to various ideas and opinions.

CHAPTER FOUR LOVE YOURSELF

3. Allow yourself to make mistakes

We're told repeatedly from a young age, "Nobody's perfect. Everyone makes mistakes," but the older you get, the more pressure you feel about not failing. Cut yourself some slack! Make mistakes so you can learn and grow from them. Embrace your past. You're constantly changing and growing from who you once were into who you are today and who you will be one day. Forget about that voice in your head (Imposter Syndrome) that says you need to be perfect. Make mistakes—make lots of them—and learn from those experiences. The lessons you'll gain are priceless. Failing is okay. It's what you learn from failing that makes you grow the most. I have failed many times, but it has helped to shape who I am today. I believe that failure is a success. I don't see failure as the end. It gives you the opportunity to learn, grow and change. It just opens the door for something greater.

4. Remember, your value doesn't lie in how your body looks

This is fundamental, and many things in the world want to distract you from this powerful truth. Sometimes even your own internalized sexism affirms your thoughts of inadequacy. You are valuable because you are *you*, not because of your body. Go ahead and wear what makes you feel good. Whether a lot or a little, wear what makes you feel confident, comfortable and happy. As you know now, my clothes were my confidence "suit of armor," but on one momentous day, I learned I didn't need designer clothes to make me feel confident. You'll read that story in an upcoming chapter.

5. Don't be afraid to let go of toxic people

Not everybody takes responsibility for the energy they put out into the world. If someone is bringing toxicity into your life and won't take responsibility for it, then that might mean you need to step away from them. Don't be afraid to do this. It's liberating and important, even though it may be painful. Surround yourself with people that build you up and support you, not those who bring you down. I spent too much time around negative people. I decided to cut them out. My circle of friends is small, but I'm okay with that. Think quality over quantity. I've realized that the older I get, the smaller the group of friends I have.

Keep the ones that matter to you the most, the closest. My friends give me such joy, and I treasure each one of them. If you have one great friend in your life, consider yourself lucky, as many people can't say that. Remember to protect your energy. It's not rude or wrong to remove yourself from situations or the company of people draining you.

6. Process your fears

Feeling afraid is natural and human. Don't reject your fears but try to understand them. This healthy exercise can help with your mental health. Interrogating and evaluating your fears helps you gain clarity and unmask issues in your life that are causing you anxiety. Processing those fears can help relieve you of that anxiety. I was so frightened during the years I was bullied. That constant feeling of being threatened, beaten and excluded was terrifying. I had to face the music and get control of it. The bullies were my secondary fear because I figured out that my actual fear was never becoming the person I wanted to be.

7. Trust yourself to make good decisions for yourself

We so often doubt ourselves and our ability to do what's right when most of the time, we know in our hearts what's best. Remember that your feelings are valid. You know yourself better than anyone else, so be your best advocate. If you know it's wrong, don't do it. You know your purpose, so serve it by serving yourself in the best way you can by living your truth.

8. Put yourself first

Don't feel bad about doing this. Women, especially, can grow accustomed to putting others first. Although there's a time and a place for this, it shouldn't be a habit that costs you your mental or emotional well-being. Find the time to decompress. Without decompressing and recharging, you can put a serious strain on yourself. Whether spending the day in bed or outdoors in nature, find what helps you decompress and dedicate time to this. Yoga helps me feel calm and centered. I also enjoy taking a walk or bike ride to clear my head. Remember that mental health day we just talked about?

9. Feel pain and joy as fully as you can

Allow yourself to feel things fully. Lean into pain, revel in your joy and don't put limitations on your feelings. Fear, pain and joy are emotions that will help you understand yourself and realize that you are not your feelings. Once I began to feel good about myself, I was able to experience happiness and joy on a whole different level. I even slept better. I also leaned on people I trusted and counted on and knew I had their support.

10. Exercise boldness in public

Get into the habit of speaking your mind. Don't wait for permission to take a seat at the table. Join the conversation. Contribute your thoughts. Take up space and own your territory. Too often, women make themselves smaller. This often happens at work meetings or while networking. Boldness is like a muscle—it grows the more you exercise it. It's okay to start small. Send back a meal that wasn't to order or speak up for what you want on a pizza when ordering in a group. Try taking "It doesn't matter" out of your vocabulary when asked what you want. What you want *does* matter. Take action and know that your voice is just as important as anyone else's. In my business as a speaker, coach and thought leader, I've learned to use my voice as a platform to share my knowledge and expertise. Now, I'm not afraid to share. I just jump right in and say it!

11. See the beauty in simple things

Try to notice at least one beautiful, small thing around you every day. Make a note of it and be grateful for it. Gratitude not only gives you perspective, but it's also essential to help you find joy. I like to have fresh flowers in my house. They truly give me joy. I enjoy walks in nature, and I love being around water. The beauty of a lake or ocean and the sounds that go with it make me happy.

12. Be kind to yourself

The world is full of harsh words and critiques—don't add yours to the mix. Speak kindly to yourself, and don't call yourself mean things. Don't let negative self-talk take over your inner voice. It erodes your confidence and stops you from reaching your potential. Negativity can make you feel like you will fail before you even start. Notice when a negative thought comes up and counter it with a positive one. Remember your daily positive affirmations and celebrate yourself. You've come so far and grown so much. Don't forget to celebrate yourself, and not only on your birthday!

KEY TAKEAWAYS

Even if you don't feel particularly powerful, think about how far you've come and how you've survived. You're here, right now, alive and powerful beyond your knowledge. And be patient with yourself. Self-love may not happen overnight. But with time, it will settle itself into your heart. Self-love is an essential nutrient in our lives. We can nourish ourselves fully by practicing self-care and self-compassion.

Self-love is essential for the growth, learning and fullness that come with living your whole truth. Yes, you may sometimes struggle and find yourself on a bumpy road. Challenges come in the form of self-doubt, fear, being too busy, distractions, a fear of being too self-indulgent, or feelings of not being worthy enough to even get started. Be patient with yourself and know that you are worth it. By detoxing your self-doubt, you'll look back on these moments and see how they were stepping stones on your journey to being the best you.

CHAPTER FOUR LOVE YOURSELF

Now, I know you're busy. You are spouses, parents, children, friends, professionals, volunteers, and household managers. But as you have just learned, practicing self-love is essential for your journey to feeling confident every day. Try to find at least 20 minutes a day just for you. Maybe it's a quick workout, reading a devotional, a cup of coffee, taking a walk, or talking with a friend. Try yoga or meditation. Whatever it may be, just do it for yourself. Paint your nails, do a puzzle or read a book. I love to get up in the morning and have my coffee. Sometimes I just sit in silence. All I know is that having that "me" time is so crucial for my well-being and growth, and it just makes me feel better! Make time for yourself a priority. I have found that when I have my "me" time, I am so much happier, and it helps me feel centered and focused.

ACTIVITY #5 – SELF-ASSESSMENT –
WHERE ARE YOU IN YOUR SELF-LOVE JOURNEY?

Read these statements and rate them on a scale of 0 to 5. When finished, add up the total score.

0= Never 1=Rarely 2=Sometimes 3=Frequently
4=Most Often 5=Always

1. I believe I am worthy and deserving of love.   _____

2. I believe I am special.   _____

3. I believe I have a purpose for living.   _____

4. I can communicate my needs and wants.   _____

5. I accept and love my body just the way it is.   _____

6. I do not need to be in a romantic relationship to feel whole. _____

7. I think it is okay to make mistakes and not be the best. _____

8. I am okay with saying "no" to things or people that don't bring me joy. _____

9. I place equal importance on my feelings as on other people's feelings. _____

10. I deserve good things in my life. _____

Scoring:

40-50 – You have achieved a wonderful sense of self-love. Keep growing and loving yourself.

30-40 – You're on your way. Keep taking time to remember you are special and important.

20-30 – There are times you feel worthy, and other times you struggle. Keep working and believing in yourself.

10-20 – You struggle to feel worthy and loved. You are in the right place to learn how to love yourself.

0-10 – It's time to build a new foundation for you to develop self-love. Keep reading—you deserve it.

Even if you scored high in the above assessment, you can still benefit from the information and activities in this book.

Self-love can change your life. The energy that can come from self-love will propel you into becoming the best version of yourself. Your self-doubt and insecurity will not trap you anymore.

CHAPTER FOUR LOVE YOURSELF

When self-worth grows from within, love blossoms and spreads to the outside world, creating more enriched and authentic relationships. When you love yourself, you will grow, thrive and achieve. You become free to make mistakes and still move about in the world, learning and experiencing life with a fresh perspective. Are you starting to feel the BLOOM?

You can learn more through observation than anything you've ever been told.
TREVA GRAVES

CHAPTER *Five*
Observation

Step 3 to Beat Your Bully and Bloom Confidence

Observation is the action or process of observing something or someone to gain information.

If you want more confidence in your life, sometimes you just need to observe the people around you. Observe their mannerisms, body language and clothing. If you're at work, take notice of how colleagues communicate, take up space and their leadership skills. I observed the confident people around me, including my friends, co-workers, bosses, and family members. I even watched people at airports and malls. I took notes and read books to educate myself on how to build myself up because I wanted to stop tearing myself down. I've worked for some great bosses who taught me how to lead with grace and humility. I've also had a couple of awful ones who exhibited traits I would never want to emulate.

By taking the time to observe and learn from others, we can build a deeper understanding of how to navigate different situations and challenges. This can help us feel more prepared and competent when faced with new experiences and give us the confidence we need to succeed.

To improve your observational skills, slow down your pace of processing information and train yourself to pay closer attention to your surroundings. You might practice mindfulness techniques, journaling or actively listening to thoroughly examine what you're hearing or seeing.

BENEFITS OF OBSERVATION

1. **Increased knowledge:** Observation helps us gain knowledge about the world, people and situations. It provides us with valuable information that can help us make better decisions and take appropriate actions. I've always believed that knowledge is power. The more you learn and experience, the better off you will be and the easier if will be to implement what you learn.

2. **Improved understanding:** By observing others, we can gain a better understanding of their thoughts, emotions and behaviors. This helps us be more empathetic and build stronger relationships with others. Our emotional intelligence (EQ) helps us to become self-aware of our actions and how we respond to relieve stress, communicate effectively, empathize with others, overcome challenges, and defuse conflict. Good EQ is an integral part of being successful on the job and in life. I can think of many times where my emotional intelligence was challenged. I've learned over the years what pushes my buttons. If you find yourself in a difficult situation, try to manage your emotions in a positive way.

3. **Enhanced problem-solving:** Observation can help us identify problems and come up with creative solutions. By observing how others approach challenges, we can learn from their strategies and apply them to our own situations. Solving problems is a basic life skill that is developed over time and is essential to our day-to-day lives. We solve problems without really thinking

about how we solve them. Problem-solving will empower you in your personal and professional life.

4. **Improved communication:** By paying attention to nonverbal cues, body language and tone of voice, we can better understand what others are trying to communicate. This can help us communicate more effectively with others and build stronger relationships. As someone who has studied and worked in the communication industry for over 25 years, I can honestly say that your communication skills are your most important defining attribute. If you aspire to be a CEO, a leader in your company, an entrepreneur, or even a keynote speaker, good communication skills are necessary for you to influence, motivate and support yourself, your employees or your team. Just watch Oprah Winfrey, Dr. Brené Brown, Tony Robbins and Daymond John. They are masters of communication.

5. **Increased self-awareness:** Observing our own thoughts, emotions and behaviors can help us gain a better understanding of ourselves. This can help us identify areas for personal growth and work on improving our weaknesses. The activities and quizzes in this book help you become more aware of your thoughts and feelings. Self-awareness is the key to your success.

6. **Enhanced critical thinking:** Observation helps us think critically and analyze situations. By paying attention to details and thinking through the implications of different actions, we can make more informed decisions. Observational skills are the starting point for critical thinking. Observant people can quickly sense and identify new problems. This skill may even be able to help you predict when a problem might occur before it happens.

7. **Better learning:** By observing and learning from others, we can improve our skills and knowledge in a variety of areas. This can

help us be more effective in our work and personal lives. Pay attention to the details, take notes and then reproduce what you observed.

ALBERT BANDURA'S 4 STAGES OF OBSERVATIONAL LEARNING

Albert Bandura is a researcher and psychologist whom people often associate with learning through observation. Although he believed people modeled the behavior they saw, he also claimed that some people learned from the behavior rather than modeled it. For example, if a child observed someone getting chastised for negative conduct, they would learn from what they saw and not repeat the behavior to avoid a similar consequence. Similarly, if they saw someone getting rewarded for something positive, they learned they could do something comparable and get rewarded. Interesting, right? Let's take a brief look at the four stages of observational learning.

1. Attention

If a person is going to learn anything from someone else, they must pay complete attention to the person and the behaviors they are exhibiting. There are a few factors that affect a person's ability to focus and give their full attention:

> **Physical similarities:** Observers sometimes pay more attention to others who are of the same sex or similar age.
>
> **Prestige:** People the learner sees as attractive, successful or distinguished are more likely to be observed and modeled by others.
>
> **Health:** If an observer is ill or tired, they may not be able to focus completely on the subject they're observing. This can impact their ability to later imitate the behavior they learned.

2. Retention

The second stage of observational learning is the ability to retain the information learned while observing. A distracted or unfocused learner is less likely to remember what they learned and may have a more challenging time repeating it. If this happens, they might need to go back to stage one and see the behavior completed again to model it.

3. Reproduction

The third stage of learning is the ability to reproduce the behavior learned through observing and retaining the information. A learner may need to try recreating the behavior multiple times before completing it successfully. Being able to reproduce the action is an important factor to consider. If you can do it successfully, you may have an excellent chance of success.

4. Motivation

Motivation is the learner's desire to learn the behavior they observe. If someone observes a behavior but isn't motivated to retain the information, they're less likely to reproduce it. There are a few motivating factors that a person can use to propel a person to perform: The intention to be successful, positive mindset and confidence.

BODY LANGUAGE

Nonverbal communication makes a powerful impression. We've all heard the saying, "Actions speak louder than words." Did you know that 93% of communication is non-verbal and only 7% of communication we exhibit is verbal? Studies show that eye contact, facial expression, gestures, and posture send more memorable messages than words. You have a lot of control over the signals you're sending, and projecting confidence isn't as difficult as you think.

Amy Cuddy is a social psychologist, bestselling author, award-winning Harvard lecturer, and keynote speaker. She focuses on presence and performance under stress, the causes and outcomes of feeling powerful vs. powerless, prejudice and stereotyping nonverbal behavior, and the delicate balance of projecting trustworthiness and strength. She popularized the idea of "power posing" or holding your body in an expansive posture for a couple of minutes before you walk into a situation that will challenge your confidence.

Try standing in the "Wonder Woman" pose with your feet shoulder-width apart, hands on your hips, while you puff your chest out. Now, she doesn't suggest you do it in front of a packed boardroom, but if you can find a private place to practice it, you will reap physiological and psychological rewards. I have practiced this, and it helps me feel more powerful. I especially do this right before a speaking engagement to help me frame my thoughts and energy, as it puts me in a confident mindset.

Postural expansion techniques include "enlarging" behaviors, such as sitting more erectly, opening the torso and extending limbs away from the body. I believe that high and low-power posing can influence your self-esteem. High-power posing is understood as the nonverbal expression of power through open, expansive body postures. In contrast, contractive and closed body postures mark low-power posing. Try high-power posing and see how it makes you feel when you are about to enter a situation where you may be uncomfortable. If you're applying for a job, it may be the difference between having a great interview or a bad one.

Practice body language that shows confidence. Walk with purpose and sit tall. Hold your head high and use good eye contact. Start small and try something new each day. Keep observing and make small changes. Remember, micro-movements! Then, when you are ready, try another posture. Confidence is like a muscle. Keep practicing and it will build over time. If you need help or examples of how body language can help you appear as a confident person, reach out to me and I will send you a free download of

CHAPTER FIVE OBSERVATION

powerful, confident body poses that will help you nail your next presentation or job interview.

Choose to "observe" and add the "O," which is the next layer of the BLOOM Framework.

ACTIVITY #6 – OBSERVATIONAL LEARNING

Observational learning is key to building confidence. We learn through this powerful tool. Observe today how people move, walk and talk. If you can, do this at a mall, the airport or the office. How do the leaders in your organization dress, move and act? How do they lead meetings? Notice how their confidence affects how they present themselves and how they are perceived. Answer these questions:

- How is their body language showing confidence? How is their posture? Are they smiling? Are they using good eye contact?
- How are they dressed? Hair? Makeup?
- How do they communicate?
- How do they sit? Stand? Walk? Gesture?
- What is the sound of their voice? Do they speak loudly? Softly? High? Low?
- Are they practicing good professional etiquette?
- Do they "own" their space?
- Is their handshake strong or weak?
- How do they treat others? Are they respectful and kind, or are they bullies?
- What kind of impression did they make?

- What can you do to improve your non-verbal confidence?
- How has the power of observation helped you see yourself differently?

Write in your journal how you will make a positive transformation in your nonverbal communication. Remember to make it a point to be aware of how you look and are perceived by those around you. Consider how your manners toward others project your confidence.

ACTIVITY #7 – WEAR SOMETHING THAT MAKES YOU FEEL CONFIDENT

Did you know that most women wear only 20% of the clothes in their closet, and 80% just hang there? That's because we go to our closet for a dose of self-esteem every day. It's time to ditch the duds and keep the gems that make you feel fabulous!

Tomorrow, wear something that makes you feel confident.

Do your hair and makeup.

Schedule a time for a closet edit. I do these in person and virtually. Let me know if you need help!

At the end of the day, consider these questions:

- Do you think people reacted to you differently by how you looked and dressed?
- Did anyone comment or give you a compliment about how you were dressed? How did that make you feel?
- Do you think clothes have an impact on how you are perceived?

Your appearance directly impacts the first impression you make or any impression for that matter. A sloppy, disheveled appearance speaks volumes about you. If you present yourself professionally

CHAPTER FIVE OBSERVATION

and "put together," you will attract others, and people will want to get to know you. The way you present yourself will long be remembered. Research says that 85% of the time, your first impression sticks—so make it a good one!

Take advantage of every opportunity in life.
TREVA GRAVES

CHAPTER Six

Opportunities

Step 4 to Beat Your Bully and Bloom Confidence

Opportunity is a set of circumstances that makes it possible to do something.

I've had a lot of wonderful opportunities come my way in life. Like most people, I've taken some and missed out on others. But taking advantage of as many opportunities as possible is important. Sometimes just one opportunity can mean the difference between an extraordinary life and a mediocre one. Inspirational Speaker Tony Robbins once said, "Expect change. Analyze the landscape. Take the opportunities. Stop being the chess piece; become the player. It's your move." He is so right!

When I turned 30, I entered the Mrs. Iowa America pageant. Thoughts of this took me back to my initial modeling days at the Bernice Johnson School of Modeling when I saw all the beautiful pictures of women on the walls in the studio. Back then, it was only something I had dreamed about. I had done a couple of pageants earlier in my teens and 20s, and I always placed runner-up. I had gained so much more confidence since then, but because this would be my last pageant, I hired a coach to help me WIN! You may think pageants are ridiculous and irrelevant today, and I can understand this perspective. Many pageants are "beauty" pageants. People ask, "Why do girls and women feel the need to go up on a stage in a swimsuit or gown and parade around looking beautiful with their hair and lash extensions, makeup and spray tans?"

It was 1998, and back then, there weren't hair extensions, and no one was getting a spray tan. The Internet was just barely coming of age, and social media wasn't even a phrase. In my opinion, the world was a better place with less stress and anxiety than it is today. I didn't participate in pageants to feel "like a beautiful queen" for a day. I did it to prove to myself that my confidence was as strong as ever. I would be lying if I said I didn't love the attention of being on a stage, wearing a beautiful gown and having my hair and makeup done. It was exhilarating! More importantly, I saw this competition as an opportunity to really push myself. Pageants taught me many life and business skills. For example, they taught me how to communicate, think on my feet, give successful interviews, lead meetings, and be a better employee.

I've been interviewed on television a hundred times, and I can honestly say, pageants helped me navigate how the media works. Appearing on television or a podcast can be terrifying if you feel insecure about yourself. I learned that an interview is just about people having a conversation, so I viewed the camera as another person I would have to look at and include in the conversation. That helped me communicate with confidence. Pageants taught me business etiquette skills and how to network better with my peers and colleagues. They also taught me I could confidently speak in front of hundreds of people. Pageants taught me how to lead, listen and learn from others. They also taught me more about taking care of myself and my body through fitness and well-being. Participating in pageants gave me the skills necessary to have the confidence to put myself out there for the world to see and be proud of. I learned that many women in pageants are intelligent, talented and gifted. Pageants are catalysts for some women to champion

CHAPTER SIX OPPORTUNITIES

causes and speak out on their platform of choice to bring attention to a topic or idea. Pageants gave me my voice and the opportunity to share it with the world.

If you are wondering what happened—yes, I won! I was crowned Mrs. Iowa America 1998. It was one of the most exciting days of my life. I went on to the national Mrs. America pageant in Las Vegas, Nevada. I was awarded the "Best State Costume" from Florence Henderson (Mrs. Brady from the Brady Bunch)! My costume was a hot air balloon since Iowa was home to the National Hot Air Balloon Museum. Getting that costume to Las Vegas was a challenge and an experience I will never forget. During the pageant, I was chosen to be Tony Marco's model during a makeup tutorial session. He handpicked me from a group of 50 women. That was pretty exciting! Tony Marco is a famous Hollywood makeup artist who worked on the movie "Titanic." He did Kate Winslet's makeup every day! The point I am trying to make is that I experienced all these incredible events because I decided to seize an opportunity.

To see an opportunity, we must be open to all thoughts. They are everywhere, and the key is to develop the vision to see them. Choose "opportunity" and add the other "O" to the next layer of the BLOOM Framework.

> *"Don't wait for the right opportunity: Create it."*
> **GEORGE BERNARD SHAW**

NINE TIPS TO HELP YOU SEIZE EVERY OPPORTUNITY

Unfortunately, opportunities that come along don't last forever. But the good news is that you can take steps to make sure you don't miss out on something truly life changing. When an opportunity presents itself, don't be afraid to go after it! The year 1998 was an exciting one for me. Not only was I crowned Mrs. Iowa America, but I was also offered the opportunity to be the first-ever Internet shopping spokesmodel for the Ritz-Carlton Hotels in the 1990s. Depending on how old you are, remember those little black boxes that sat on the desk in hotel rooms? All you had to do was push a button on that box to shop and purchase anything from toothbrushes to clothes and even luggage. I was sort of the "Price is Right" spokesmodel on their private shopping service where I showcased items you could buy from the hotel. Those black boxes are a thing of the past, but it was another opportunity that came my way, and I seized it!

Here are some tips to help you seize the moment and take advantage of opportunities that could very well change your life.

1. Say "yes" more often

Taking advantage of opportunities in life starts with simply saying "yes" to them when they come around. When I decided I wanted to get more involved in my community, I was asked to volunteer to lead a committee of people and organize a Walk for Multiple Sclerosis. My interest in MS started when I was working as a speech pathologist in a hospital and met a woman with the disease who was my age. We had an immediate connection, and I wanted to learn more about it. I had no other ties to MS other than this patient I treated at the hospital.

It ignited a passion in me to help people with disabilities. This volunteer opportunity led me to many other leadership roles within the MS organization. I was asked to be on the MS Clinical Advisory Board for the State of South Dakota, headed up large-scale projects, emceed events, and was eventually honored with being chosen as the Honorary Chair for the State of South Dakota MS Walk. It was truly an honor! All of this happened because of an opportunity I saw to get involved. It touched me in so many ways. I became a better volunteer, a better leader and a better person

CHAPTER SIX OPPORTUNITIES

from that experience, and it is one I will never forget. I also made new friends from those experiences that I still have to this day.

Great opportunities often come from your great ideas, so don't say "no." If you're holding negative thoughts about yourself, you'll limit your options. This is not a good state of mind. Taking advantage of opportunities simply means saying "yes." Initially, you may feel unsure of yourself, but the more risks you take to get outside your comfort zone, the more you grow, and your self-confidence will soar.

2. Don't hesitate

Opportunities are, by definition, short-lived. You need to be quick to get the most out of them. For example, I've known many men who hesitated to talk to women they were attracted to. They waited for the right time to make their move. However, as they were waiting for the right time, someone else would meet her first. Opportunities are not always exclusive to you. Others might be tempted to move in on them if they see them. If you hesitate, you may lose out. Take a step back and ask yourself, "Does it serve my purpose?" "How would I feel if I let this opportunity go?" "Would it make me happy or stress me out?" If the answers to those questions are positive, then don't hesitate. Just do it!

3. Take more risks

Opportunities and risk-taking often go together. And the best ones are often the riskiest. Someone starting up a new business is not only taking a risk but also taking advantage of an opportunity. When I started my business in 2013, it was risky but exciting, and I had very little money to invest in it. But I knew I would regret it if I didn't do it. Sometimes you must do something that makes you afraid to experience personal growth. I started small as an image consultant, but each year my business grew. It led me to take on new opportunities to help serve women not only with their image but their communication skills, leadership, business etiquette, and career skills. Today, I am a personal brand expert with two degrees and ten professional certifications. Eventually, I added coaching and speaking and then wrote two books—which I never thought I would do. This book is my third. Who knows what lies ahead for me? All I know is that I took advantage of or created opportunities for myself to grow and learn so that I could help other people do the same. Those opportunities built my confidence.

Think back to a time when you were sitting on a couch watching television. How many opportunities came your way? Probably none, right? Watching TV is low risk and offers few opportunities. Sometimes, you must jumpstart those opportunities with a risk or two.

4. Have a positive attitude

Having a positive attitude has several advantages. For one, it helps you succeed when you're taking a risk. When I started my new business, how far would I have gotten if I was negative during setbacks or if I only foresaw failure? I wouldn't be successful, that's for sure. Having a positive attitude about your chances of success can give you added confidence. I have failed in a business or two that I have started. I failed because I didn't give it the time and energy that goes into being successful.

Sometimes I lost interest, and sometimes life just got too busy. Maybe it wasn't the right time or not important enough for me to work hard. I found my passion career later in life, and it's what I'm doing now. It energizes me every day to get up and work with people to build confidence and create amazing personal brands. I love coaching and speaking, and certainly, writing this book was something I was excited to do! It all has to do with attitude and how much you want something.

5. Meet more people

When it comes to opportunities, it's often who you know rather than what you know. Imagine, for a moment, someone looking for a job. One person has a network of five close friends and a

CHAPTER SIX OPPORTUNITIES

few acquaintances, and another has 30 friends and many acquaintances. If their qualifications are identical, it's much more likely that the person who knows more people will get hired first.

Why is that? The person with more friends has a larger network. More jobs are found through networking than online job postings. Join LinkedIn or start your own community on Facebook or another platform. If you are looking for work or volunteer opportunities or just want to network with people who share a hobby like yours, go for it! The opportunities are there; you just may have to search for them. And wouldn't it be fun to meet and connect with people who have the same interests as you?

6. Be curious

Curiosity awakens your mind and keeps it active. Curious people ask a lot of questions and search for answers. Eventually, you may ask a question no one else has asked before. Answer that question, and you'll come up with a new idea. By asking a lot of questions about the world, you get a better understanding of it. Don't be a passive player. Try and figure out why things are the way they are. If you don't like the answer, use your voice, and change it! Being a catalyst for change is very empowering.

7. Focus

Know what you want out of life. If you know what you want out of life, your mind will focus on that and be on the lookout when an opportunity arises. This also helps when determining the direction of your life. When I decided to start my own business, I was terrified. I didn't know if people would see me as a professional who could help them. I was focused on creating an opportunity that I could get paid for to create the life I wanted. I found it in helping people detox their self-doubt and have confidence in their life, along with taking that confidence they now have and building an image and personal brand to support it. I am living my passion, and it feels so good.

Now, not everyone can take a passion and turn it into a business but doing what you love, whether it's your job or a hobby, helps you remain happy, engaged and content. I started my entrepreneurial journey later than most. Never worry about being too old to focus on your career goals. It doesn't matter if you are in your 40s, 50s, 60s or beyond. It's also never too early. Hear that, 20-somethings? Jump in and give it your best shot!

8. Make decisions and stick with them

The flip side to being focused is having no focus at all. Many people don't have opportunities simply because they don't make any decisions. It's always possible to make the wrong decision, but a wrong decision is still better than no decision at all. When I decided to go to graduate school to get my communication degree, I was hesitant at first. I had debated doing it for years, and I wasn't sure if I could even afford it. However, I decided to make a decision and stick with it. Now, I just wish I had done it when I first considered it. Education is something that can never be taken away from you and helps you become a well-rounded person. It challenges you. In my opinion, learning never really ends. It continues throughout your life whether you have a degree hanging on your wall or not.

Whether or not you were productive, Friday eventually makes its way to you every week. If you're like me, you look back at your week and think about what you accomplished and what you could have accomplished. Some weeks are more productive than others, but every day we have the chance to make decisions and take advantage of opportunities in front of us. Remember to speak kindly to yourself and not dwell on the "could haves."

9. Take every opportunity life presents or create your own

The timing will never be perfect for that next big step in your life. The setup may not be ideal, but that shouldn't hold you back from reaching to meet your goals and dreams. Instead, seize the moment. Take advantage of opportunities that support your journey.

CHAPTER SIX OPPORTUNITIES

Because I was so fearful in my young life, I didn't take advantage of opportunities that I should have.

> *"If the opportunity doesn't knock, build a door."*
> **MILTON BERLE**

ACTIVITY #8 – TAKE ADVANTAGE OF A NEW OPPORTUNITY

Take advantage of one new opportunity this week. Join a committee or volunteer for a cause or passion of yours. Take the lead on a project at work, start your community on social media or create something new on your own. Whether it's a large opportunity or a small one, just say "yes." It will help you expand your horizons and grow your self-confidence.

Questions to consider:

- What have you learned about yourself through this process? Stay alert as an opportunity may come along, and you may not even realize it.

- Even if you are just a little interested, do it! It may open a door for you that you never expected.

- Did the opportunity scare you or bring you joy and satisfaction?

Mentors can change your life.
TREVA GRAVES

CHAPTER *Seven*

Mentor

Step 5 to Beat Your Bully and Bloom Confidence

A mentor is an experienced or trusted advisor. When my mother signed me up for modeling and confidence classes, I had no idea the impact that Bernice Johnson and Janet May would have on me. They greatly influenced me and my confidence throughout my life. These two phenomenal women were not only modeling instructors but confidence miracle workers for me and coached me on how to feel good about myself. They gave me the tools to become confident and believe in myself and my self-worth. They were my first mentors.

As I began my professional life, I trusted select friends and bosses who also became mentors. They provided guidance and support in my work and personal life. They helped me make tough decisions about which path to take when struggling. My mentors had my best interests at heart and gave me quality time and the benefit of their experience that I needed. My husband has also been a mentor, even though sometimes I have disagreed with him. He's given me advice I didn't necessarily *want* to hear but *needed* to hear. That's what a good mentor does. They help you hear and see both sides of what you are thinking, which improves your problem-solving skills. Mentors can also help you increase your confidence by helping you develop leadership skills. Research shows that having a mentor is beneficial to your overall emotional health.

> "A mentor is someone who sees more talent and ability within you, than you see in yourself, and helps bring it out of you."
>
> **BOB PROCTOR**

I believe in "paying it forward," so one of my favorite things to do is mentoring teen girls looking to build their confidence and self-esteem. When I help any young person defeat self-doubt and insecurity, that's a great day for me. Since I've been in that horrible space as a teen, I know exactly how young girls feel if they are being bullied or experiencing low self-esteem. With social media so prevalent today, cyberbullying has become the primary way bullies express their power. We must look for ways to work together to defeat bullies for good, and I believe mentors can help with this task.

I have had many other mentors in my life. I didn't even consider calling them mentors because they were good friends who always listened to and supported me. You may have had a mentor who is a friend or family member who has helped you in the past. I think it's a good idea to find someone who isn't necessarily a part of your life and who can give you solid guidance and encouragement with a fresh pair of eyes and ears.

Let's look at how to find a great mentor and add the "M" to the last layer of the BLOOM Framework.

CHAPTER SEVEN MENTOR

THE THREE A'S OF MENTORSHIP

The three A's to finding a great mentor comprise active listening, availability and analysis. When you work with your coach or mentor, you should experience these three A's working in tandem. If your mentor is professional and well-trained, you will feel you're in safe hands and will gain the value you need for yourself.

1. Active Listening

Mentorship requires active listening as a foundational approach to you. Active listening is an acquired skill that isn't formally taught in school classrooms. Still, it makes up about 45% of communication, so perhaps it should be. Active listening benefits you because your mentor stops talking and starts listening to you. All their attention is on what you are about to say, and they are waiting to respond by drawing on their depth of knowledge and experience.

- **Guides the Conversation**

  A good mentor guides the conversation as if sailing a boat. They try to avoid yes/no questions. Instead, they look for the open waters of discovery. To do this, they use broad queries to suggest possible directions and outcomes for clients. Often, it's not the mentor's job to offer advice and solutions; rather, they facilitate self-discovery. This was so true for me. Bernice and Janet guided me to solve some of my insecurities and problems rather than just telling me what to do. That strategy is excellent because it builds self-confidence. One of my great bosses early in my career also challenged me to look within myself for answers. Often you have the answer already. You may just need a little guidance from your mentor to find it.

- **Pays Attention and Offers Feedback**

  A mentor should always employ active listening in your sessions together, and you will feel the benefits of it even if you

are unaware of the action. Nevertheless, you also need to know the mentor is listening and understanding, as this is where summary and feedback come in. Often, your mentor will sum up what you say to reassure you they have understood correctly. Quality feedback follows this close attention.

2. Availability

When you work with a mentor, they should make themselves available in several ways. You should be able to meet up with them in person, of course, but you also need to have confidence in their emotional engagement with you. Maybe your mentor is a trusted friend or boss. Having them available for you to call on, especially when you need them, is something to consider. This is your time, and it's your chance to pick their brain. Also, it's important to notice their body language and how they conduct themselves. Is their body language open and inviting or closed off? Watch for those cues.

3. Analysis – Honesty with Diplomacy

As with most people today, time is limited, and you want to get the most value from your time with your mentor as possible. A good mentor won't beat around the bush. They will dispense with formalities and target the issue. It might be uncomfortable, but it's the best mode of analysis. I've always liked direct mentors who get to the point rather than sugarcoating something. I like mentors to shoot straight from the hip!

Objectivity and fairness are vital to having and building a solid mentor-mentee relationship. A strong mentor has walked this path before, so they know what to look for and where the shortcuts are. They take you out of your world and help you see new perspectives, even if those are uncomfortable at first. Remember, good mentors also have empathy and provide encouragement, which leads to persistence and resilience and use affirmations to help someone see the

CHAPTER SEVEN MENTOR

good in themselves. They have a vision and can see a bold future for you. They help you set goals so you get something done every day.

Mentors see life as a process of development. It starts with an orientation toward serving and supporting someone else. It emerges from an emotion of care or love. Mentoring is also about inspiration and support and will help you transform your life to a higher level and develop life skills that you can use every day in any relationship.

> *"A mentor is someone who allows you to see the hope inside yourself."*
> **OPRAH WINFREY**

The bottom line here is that mentors should support your growth, whether it is for personal or professional development. They should help you set goals and give honest feedback. They should serve as a source of knowledge for you and provide specific insights and information that enable your success. Mentors should help you set your goals and help you be accountable for them. Having a mentor in your life can motivate you to keep working on your goals.

Great mentors offer encouragement and support to help you keep moving forward despite your challenges. They should instill a sense of confidence in you, so you don't give up on your goals. In other words, they keep you on track for success! I've also had mentors who provided connections and have helped me build my professional network. This can be invaluable to you for your professional growth. They are good listeners and become trusted allies who have your best interests at heart. Getting their feedback is imperative, and helping you identify your strengths and weaknesses is a great way to improve yourself. Communication is key!

Mentors can also help set professional guidelines and expectations. Since your mentor should have a good amount of experience in their background, they can be an excellent free resource to help you grow and establish a more authentic and personal connection. They genuinely want to help you be successful and become a confident person. Having a mentor in your life may continue for a few months or for years. Mentoring is a learning relationship, usually focused on long-term career development, but the goal is for you to become the master of yourself. Your turn may come at some point to be a mentor for someone else. I do what I do now so I can give back and mentor others, and I've never been happier showing them the open door to their greatness!

ACTIVITY #9 – TEN PROFESSIONAL MENTORING ACTIVITIES TO CONSIDER

Seek a mentor that can help guide you on your journey to confidence. I have included some tips here to consider as you look for a mentor. To find the right person, interview them. Take him/her out for coffee and ask some questions I listed below. Work with the right one who fits your values. How does he/she make you feel when you are with them? Meet at least monthly. I truly believe everyone should have a mentor who can be a sounding board for you to learn from and engage with. Maybe it's a trusted friend. Perhaps it's a boss or someone outside of your professional network. Learning never really ends, and the more information and coaching you can soak up, the better prepared you will be for all life's challenges.

- Kick off your mentoring relationship with coffee or lunch.
- Have a goal-planning session.
- Create a vision statement together.
- Do a mutual job shadow.

CHAPTER SEVEN MENTOR

- Roleplay.
- Discuss goal-related news or events.
- Read a book together.
- Attend a virtual or physical conference together.
- Conduct a resume revision session.
- If you are already a mentor, create a networking event for your mentee.

QUESTIONS TO ASK A MENTOR

- What's the best advice you can give to help plan a career rather than simply work to keep a job?
- How do you encourage innovative ideas?
- How would you describe your style?
- Do you have a mentor? How have they influenced you?
- What do you do to constantly challenge your underlying beliefs and assumptions?
- Would you do anything differently if given the opportunity?
- How and where do you find inspiration?
- How do you keep your feelings separate from your decision-making?
- What values are you committed to?
- How do you balance your work and home life?
- Do you have any books you suggest I read?

SUCCESSFUL MENTORING SESSIONS

- Prepare and ask relevant questions.
- Be respectful of your mentor's time and experience.
- Ask if you can follow up and exchange contact information.
- Afterward, ask yourself what you learned from the meeting and how you can apply your new knowledge.
- Thank your mentor for their advice with an email or personalized note.

Once you have a mentor, remember to take notes or journal about each session and what you learned from it. Write down your strengths, weaknesses and goals and keep track of your progress. Review these with your mentor and see how much you have changed and grown over time. Mentors help you become the person you want to be and live confidently and with purpose.

Congratulations! You did it!

You have learned the 5 Steps to Beat Your Bully to move forward and BLOOM Confidence. The next chapter will focus on maintaining self-confidence and gaining a deeper appreciation for your unique self. True confidence is achieved when you have gained self-worth.

Your self-worth comes from truly embracing who you are.
TREVA GRAVES

CHAPTER *Eight*
Self-Worth

Self-worth is the feeling that you are a good person who deserves to be treated with respect.

I've mentioned a few times in this book that designer clothes became my "confidence suit of armor." But, I'm happy to say, there was a day when things changed for me. Here is my story of the life-changing day when I emotionally felt I didn't need designer clothes to cover up my self-doubt.

My entire life, I used clothes and my "perfect" appearance to cover up my deep internal insecurities, and girls were jealous of me. It was why I was bullied so much as a child and teen. They wanted my external "fake" persona. I could fake a smile, in fact, fake a lot of things, but I couldn't fake having confidence. You can see through fake. You can see it in a person's eyes, in their body language and movement. I had spent the last 13 years practicing everything you've read in this book. I was 28 years old, standing in the dressing room at Macy's department store, and something unexpected happened.

At that time in my life, I was feeling happy and good about myself. I was just about to start graduate school, had a boyfriend I loved and friends I enjoyed spending time with. I also felt that confidence was building inside of me, and it was a wonderful feeling.

My life seemed to be "normal" for once. I had some plans for the weekend with friends and went shopping to look for some new clothes for the occasion. I found some jeans, grabbed some tops, a jean jacket, a white t-shirt and made my way to the dressing room.

First, I put on a pair of jeans and then the white t-shirt. I was going to layer it with another designer top or the jean jacket. As I turned around to look at myself in the mirror, I noticed a reflection that seemed unfamiliar to me. An unusual feeling rushed through my body when I realized it was me in the reflection, but a "simple" version of me. I felt vulnerable and exposed as I stood there, stripped down to only a white t-shirt and jeans. A little voice in my head said, "Treva, just wear the white t-shirt. That's all you need now." Those two sentences changed my life.

At that moment, I was suddenly reminded of a time when I was in 6th grade, and a girl asked me, "Why do you always wear such nice clothes to school? Why can't you just wear a t-shirt and jeans like everyone else?" I didn't answer her that day, but on this day, I had a moment of healing, and I answered the voice and said, "Yes, I can just wear a t-shirt and jeans like everyone else!" I realized I could look good, be comfortable, confident and be okay, internally and externally, in a white t-shirt and jeans. I no longer needed to hide under beautiful clothes to cover up my self-doubt. I finally felt like I had achieved a level of self-confidence that I had never felt before.

This epiphany was so powerful, yet it was revealed in such an ordinary way. The white t-shirt was the only thing I bought. I felt I could finally just be me, Treva, the woman who worked so hard to detox her self-doubt and feel confident in her own skin. I felt simple, bare, stripped down to the "fabric" of who I am—and I felt okay. I walked out of Macy's feeling like a million dollars in a $15 t-shirt.

All the years of hard work, therapy, believing in myself, practicing self-love, taking advantage of opportunities, observing people, and having mentors finally paid off. I now believed I was worthy

CHAPTER EIGHT SELF-WORTH

of love and acceptance. I accepted myself for who I was. I realized I wanted to please myself rather than be validated by everyone else. I decided to choose myself first. It was an incredibly empowering moment. This wasn't about the white t-shirt but the simplicity it stood for. I no longer needed designer armor.

The white t-shirt symbolized freedom to me. Freedom to be authentically me and feel good about it. It represented the end of fear and that the need to look and be perfect on the outside wasn't there anymore. I didn't need a mask to hide under or use clothes as a confidence "suit of armor" to cover myself up. In a simple, practical way, it all came to fruition. It came in the form of a simple white t-shirt that meant acceptance of myself and, although flawed, I'm okay. It meant that I could be my authentic self on the inside and outside and not worry if people liked me or not. I am okay with myself, no matter what. A calm, peaceful presence came over me.

When I got to my car, I sat behind the steering wheel and cried. I finally felt at peace with myself. All the work I had completed in my journey to self-confidence helped me understand I am worthy of happiness, love, acceptance, and success. My white t-shirt moment was pivotal for me in its simplicity. It took me years to understand and accept my self-worth, but I was finally there.

When you realize your self-worth, it can change your life forever. You don't need to cover up your insecurities anymore. Understanding your value and self-worth means believing in who you are as a person, accepting yourself, and never undervaluing yourself for anyone or anything. I choose to own my power and not give it away to anyone or anything else. If a bully tries to creep into my thoughts or life, I think about what BLOOM means to me and the strategies I developed to power myself through it. My bullies no longer define me. I defeated them forever.

I began to view myself as God's creation. He made all of you special and unique, and you have so much to offer. This is a way to feel your sense of value and purpose. My strengths and gifts are mine, and yours are yours. We all have unique "ingredients."

I hope I have inspired you to wear a white t-shirt with confidence and pride. Let it symbolize the freedom to be you, no matter what! My "white t-shirt" moment had such an impact on me that I created an "authentically me" white t-shirt for everyone to wear. I often wear mine as a visible, tangible reminder that when I am stripped down to my bare authentic self, I'm okay being me. I also wear it as a reminder of the journey I'm on every day to feel fabulous and be a confident woman! You can get yours at www.bloompersonalbranding.com/resources.

WHAT IS THE MEANING OF SELF-WORTH AND SELF-VALUE?

Self-worth and self-value are two related terms that are often used interchangeably. Courtney Ackerman, M.A. from positivepsychology.com/self-worth/ describes the differences this way: Having a sense of self-worth means that you value yourself. It is thinking and feeling that "I am of value. I am loveable, necessary to this life and of incomprehensible worth." Self-value is related to how you act to show that you value yourself. An action that shows you have self-value is that you stop associating with people who don't value you.

WHAT DETERMINES SELF-WORTH?

When I was young, I tried so hard to "fit in" with my peers. I wanted to be loved and accepted. I tried so hard to look good in person but also on paper. I pushed myself to succeed, as I felt I had something to prove. I wanted everyone to know I was smart and had something to offer rather than being seen as weak and insecure. I didn't want to just fade into the background. I wanted to stand out, so I set out to succeed. I eventually learned that overachieving was a coping strategy for people who felt like me. I was the first person in my immediate and extended family to earn a bachelor's degree, but I didn't stop there. Not only did I earn a master's degree, I paid for

CHAPTER EIGHT SELF-WORTH

every cent of my education myself. It felt amazing to walk across that stage at the University of South Dakota, graduating cum laude in my cap and gown with special ribbons.

I worked two and three jobs at a time to support myself. After graduating with my business and communication degrees, I really wanted to project a positive image, put some money in the bank, hang out with the "cool" people, and rise to the top. So, while I passed on a doctorate, I went on to obtain ten specialized certifications in business and personal development. After doing all of this, spending lots of money, and gaining many more valuable skills and knowledge, I took a step back, and this unsettling thought entered my mind: Did I do this for myself? Did I do it for someone or something else? Did I do it to please my parents? Or to prove to the world I was intelligent and worthy of success? I suppose it was a combination of all those things.

Although I am proud of my academic success, I realized it did not prove my self-worth to anyone, including me. When I started achieving, I thought I needed degrees, accomplishments, board appointments, and awards on my walls to prove I was smart, skilled and had value and worth. I wanted admiration for my success and intelligence. The problem was that I was looking for acceptance and self-worth from others. I was looking for external approval and value rather than looking inward.

> *"If you are looking for self-worth in others, you will never find it."*
> **TREVA GRAVES**

Self-worth isn't wrapped up in your external identity or your appearance. It's not the clothes you wear, the size you are or the attention you receive from others. It's not in how much money you make or the car you drive. It's also not who you know and their status, but the quality of the people you know and have in your circle. Your cheerleaders, remember? It's not about what you do for a living or the awards and degrees hanging on your wall. It's most certainly not about likes, followers and a large social media following.

I realized I wasn't valuing "me." Self-worth comes from genuinely engaging with the relationship you have with yourself. It's a feeling of "I have authentic value by just being me and honoring that relationship with integrity." When you begin to think about and appreciate yourself on a deeper level, you begin to understand what you're made of. It's your DNA. It's what makes you "unique."

I had to consider these questions:

What makes me happy?

What are my strengths? My gifts?

What are my weaknesses?

What are my passions?

What is my purpose in life?

What do I really want?

Why do I do what I do?

How do I get what I want?

What *do* I want?

Writing this book was therapy for me. Experiences I had pushed away and avoided to keep negative feelings out of my mind for years came flooding back. It was time for me to delve deep into myself and understand what had happened to me and why I am like I am.

Realizing your self-worth is about taking responsibility for yourself and owning up to the good and the bad. I have learned if

CHAPTER EIGHT SELF-WORTH

I make a mistake, I can accept it and not degrade myself for it. No one else gets to decide my value.

I've learned to be comfortable being me. I have a sense of value in how I interact in my personal life and business. I take part in work that is satisfying and engages me. I'm more committed to my career than ever and have created a brand for myself that I can be proud of every single day. I'm always trying to elevate my best self! I know you can do this as well.

I've also learned to set boundaries and let others know how I want to be treated. This is something I didn't do when I was bullied. I let go of my power and worth. I gave it away. Now I know how to put myself first—and that it's okay to think that way. I know now that I make a difference in the world by believing in myself and the impact that I have made and will continue to make. My knowledge and experience matter. It's how I serve others. That's my self-worth.

Low self-worth has many consequences. I know many who have felt this way and still do through the work I do with my clients. The risky behavior I exhibited when I was struggling along with tolerating abusive treatment and that nagging sense of failure that you won't reach your true potential are some of the signs.

I've learned that low self-worth is the cause, not the effect of hardships in my life—whether financial, relational or physical. You can change these feelings by changing your thoughts using the 5 Steps of BLOOM that I shared with you. Here is a recap and a few other thoughts for you to consider.

Remember:

- You are always worthy of love. Accept the God of your understanding into your heart. That God loves you no matter what.
- Things do not define you.
- It's okay not to feel "happy" every day.

- It's okay to be alone. This one can be really challenging. If this is true for you, you're doing great!

- Put your needs first. This is not selfish! You can't pour from an empty cup.

- Have gratitude every day. Be grateful for what you have.

- Detach your worthiness from achievements and external circumstances.

- Give yourself some grace. Be on your own team.

- Less is more. As I've gotten older, this is so true for me. Life is less complicated living with less and has led me to feel happier and healthier!

- Write in your journal. It helps to clear your mind when you put pen to paper. Reflect on it later to see how far you've come.

- Share your story. How will you tell it? The way you think influences the way you live. What are you going to say about yourself? Be authentic and speak your truth.

The world needs you at your fullest potential. Commit yourself to improving your self-worth, and you will feel stronger, happier and healthier. A sense of purpose and happiness will grow inside you as it did for me. Take some intentional steps to get started. Reach out to me if you need some help. Good luck!

ACTIVITY #10 – DEVELOP YOUR SELF-WORTH

Here are five activities and exercises for developing self-worth from positivepsychology.com/self-worth/. According to author and self-growth guru Adam Sicinski, there are five vital exercises for developing and maintaining self-worth. He lays them out in five stages,

CHAPTER EIGHT SELF-WORTH

but there's no need to keep them in strict order. It's fine to move back and forth or revisit stages.

1. Increase your self-understanding

Imagine that everything you have is suddenly taken away from you (i.e., possessions, relationships, friendships, status, job/career, accomplishments, achievements, etc.). Ask yourself the following questions:

a. What if everything I have was suddenly taken away from me?

b. What if all I had left was just myself?

c. How would that make me feel?

d. What would I have that would be of value?

Think about your answers to these questions and see if you can come to this conclusion: "No matter what happens externally and no matter what's taken away from me, I'm not affected internally."

Next, get to know yourself on a deeper level with these questions:

a. Who am I? I am…I am not…

b. How am I?

c. How am I in the world?

d. How do others see me?

e. How do others speak about me?

f. What key life moments define who I am today?

g. What brings me the most passion, fulfillment, and joy?

Many of these questions are related to personal branding. How you are perceived by others gives you a good perspective from the people around you. But how do you see yourself? Where these two concepts collide is where your personal brand lives. Remember, you control the impression you make, but your community controls your brand.

Once you have a good understanding of who you are and what fulfills and satisfies you, it's time to look at what isn't so great or easy about being you. Ask yourself these questions:

a. Where do I struggle most?

b. Where do I need to improve?

c. What fears often hold me back?

d. What habitual emotions hurt me?

e. What mistakes do I tend to make?

f. Where do I tend to consistently let myself down?

Finally, take a moment to look at the flip side and ask yourself:

a. What abilities do I have?

b. What am I really good at?

Spend some time on each step, but especially on the steps that remind you of your worth and your value as a person (e.g., the strengths step).

2. Boost your self-acceptance

Once you have a better idea of who you are, the next step is to enhance your acceptance of yourself.

CHAPTER EIGHT SELF-WORTH

Think of any struggles, needs for improvement, mistakes, and bad habits you have, and commit to forgiving yourself and accepting yourself without judgment or excuses.

Think about everything you learned about yourself and repeat these statements:

> I accept the good, the bad, and the ugly.
>
> I fully accept every part of myself, including my flaws, fears, behaviors, and qualities I might not be too proud of.
>
> This is how I am, and I am at peace with that.

3. Enhance your self-love

Now that you have worked on accepting yourself for who you are, you can begin to build love and care for yourself. I shared my feelings about self-love in an earlier chapter. Make it a goal to extend yourself kindness, tolerance, generosity, and compassion.

To boost self-love, start paying attention to the tone you use with yourself. Commit to being more positive and uplifting when talking to yourself.

If you're not sure how to get started, think (or say aloud) these simple statements:

> I feel valued and special.
>
> I love myself wholeheartedly.
>
> I am valuable, I am capable and I am worth it! (This is my favorite affirmation and I say it often!)

4. Recognize your self-worth

When you understand, accept, and love yourself, you will reach a point where you no longer depend on people, accomplishments, or other external factors for your self-worth.

At this point, the best thing you can do is recognize your worth and appreciate yourself for the work you've done to get here, as well as continue to maintain your self-understanding, self-acceptance, self-love, and self-worth.

To recognize your self-worth, remind yourself of these 4 things:

a. You no longer need to please other people.

b. No matter what people do or say, and regardless of what happens outside of you, you alone control how you feel about yourself.

c. You have the power to respond to events and circumstances based on your internal sources, resources, and resourcefulness, which are the reflection of your true value.

d. Your value comes from inside, from an internal measure that you've set for yourself.

5. Take responsibility for yourself

In this stage, you will practice being responsible for yourself, your circumstances, and your problems. Take full responsibility for everything that happens to you without giving your power away. Own your power and keep it in your heart. Your self-respect should always matter. Acknowledge that you have the personal power to change and influence the events and circumstances of your life. Remind yourself of what you have learned through all of these exercises and know that you hold the power in your own life. Revel in your well-earned sense of self-worth. Do you want to maintain your progress?

Here are some special worksheets and exercises to help with that!

CHAPTER EIGHT SELF-WORTH

SELF-WORTH WORKSHEET

The worksheet lists 15 statements and instructs you to rate your belief in each one on a scale from 0 (not at all) to 10 (totally or completely). The statements are:

0-1-2-3-4-5-6-7-8-9-10

I believe in myself. _____

I am just as valuable as other people. _____

I would rather be me than someone else. _____

I am proud of my accomplishments. _____

I feel good when I get compliments. _____

I can handle criticism. _____

I am good at solving problems. _____

I love trying new things. _____

I respect myself. _____

I like the way I look. _____

I love myself even when others reject me. _____

I know my positive qualities. _____

I focus on my successes and not my failures. _____

I'm not afraid to make mistakes. _____

I am happy to be me. _____

Add up all the ratings for these 15 statements to get your total score, then rate your overall sense of self-esteem on a scale from 0 (I completely dislike who I am) to 10 (I completely like who I am). Finally, ask yourself, "What would need to change for me to move up one point on the rating scale?" For example, if you rated yourself a 6, what would need to happen for you to be at a 7? You may see something here that surprises you. Take note and commit to believing in the value of who you are and what you bring to the world.

MY STRENGTHS AND QUALITIES WORKSHEET

For each of the eight sections, there are three spaces to respond. However, if you have more than three things to write down, feel free to do so. Be proud of your strengths and don't be afraid to share them with others. If you can serve just one person, you are making a difference!

The sections are:

Things I am good at:

1.

2.

3.

What I like about my appearance:

1.

2.

3.

CHAPTER EIGHT SELF-WORTH

I've helped others by:

1.

2.

3.

What I value the most:

1.

2.

3.

Compliments I have received:

1.

2.

3.

Challenges I have overcome:

1.

2.

3.

Things that make me unique:

1.

2.

3.

Times I've made others happy:

1.

2.

3.

MEDITATIONS TO BOOST SELF-WORTH

If you're a fan of meditations, google these and check out four of my favorites aimed at boosting self-worth:

A Guided Meditation to Help Quiet Self-Doubt and Boost Confidence from Health.com

Guided Meditation for Inner Peace and Self-Worth from Linda Hall

Guided Meditation: Self-Esteem from The Honest Guys Meditations & Relaxations

Increase Self-Confidence and Self-Worth, a Guided Meditation from Tracks to Relax Sleep

30-DAY JOURNAL ACTIVITY

Experts say that if you do something for 30 days, it will become a habit. Here is a sample of a journal entry you can use each day to help you check in with yourself and keep you on track. I use this!

Date: _____

Morning Check In: How Am I Feeling?

How would I like to feel?

What needs to happen for me to feel that way?

CHAPTER EIGHT SELF-WORTH

What am I committed to achieving or taking action on today?

What is my self-care activity?

What is my mantra?

Night-Time Check-In: What Went Well Today?

What did I learn or what will I do differently next time?

What am I grateful for?

POWERFUL WOMEN PLAYLIST

As a teen, I loved making cassette tapes with some of my favorite songs to motivate me. I labeled one of them Powerful Women.

Why not make yourself a playlist of songs that inspire self-love with your own soundtrack? Try playing the music in the background while working, cleaning your house or when you just need a pick-me-up. Music can be a powerful tool to inspire you and improve your attitude!

Here are some powerful fun songs to include on your playlist!

"I Will Survive" – Gloria Gaynor
"Beautiful" – Christina Aguilera
"Fight Song" – Rachel Platten
"Just Fine" – Mary J. Blige

SELF-DOUBT DETOX

"Girl On Fire" – Alicia Keys
"Born This Way" – Lady Gaga
"I'm Every Woman" – Chaka Khan
"Good as Hell" – Lizzo
"Respect" – Aretha Franklin
"9 to 5" – Dolly Parton
"Independent Woman" – Destiny's Child
"I Am Woman" – Helen Reddy
"Superwoman" – Karyn White
"Free Your Mind" – En Vogue
"Confident" – Demi Lovato
"Hit Me With Your Best Shot" – Pat Benatar
"Scrubs" – TLC
"I'm Coming Out" – Diana Ross
"Ladies First" – Queen Latifa
"Man! I Feel Like a Woman" – Shania Twain
"Brave" – Sara Bareilles
"Express Yourself" – Madonna
"Fighter" – Christina Aguilera
"Nasty" – Janet Jackson
"Sisters Are Doin' It For Themselves" – Eurythmics & Aretha Franklin

---

Write down some songs for your power playlist here:

1.

2.

3.

Conclusion

I have overcome and survived a lot in my life. Much of it, I kept to myself. I didn't want anyone to know about the physical attacks, mistakes, struggles with self-confidence or that I experienced post-traumatic stress disorder (PTSD). But I feel now is the time to tell my story. Maybe it can help or inspire you to keep trying and take the essential steps to reach your goal. My goal was to release fear and detox my self-doubt to become self-confident. Whatever you are experiencing or feeling today that holds you back, let it go. You can do it. If you can't do it alone, ask for help, like I did.

It wasn't easy to move past my traumatic events to achieve my goals. Sometimes I still feel triggered, but these events eventually led me to who I am today and what I have accomplished since then. I am no longer the weak, insecure person I once was. I now choose to live boldly without living in fear of not pleasing the people around me and continually letting myself down. I have self-worth and no longer think I must be perfect to be accepted. I accept myself as is. I also choose to live a life with no regrets. If I see something that interests me, I want to learn more about it. I'm not afraid to take a risk or put myself out there. I'm not afraid of failure, which is such an empowering feeling. Failure is just another opportunity to learn and try something new. The power of positive thinking, a change in mindset and believing in myself altered the course of my life. It can alter yours, too.

I worked hard to earn my B.A. in Business Management and M.A. in Communication Disorders and ten specialized certifications. I became a model, commercial actress and pageant winner. I travel the country speaking on topics that I am passionate about, and I have published two books on image and personal branding. This book is my third. Finally, I started my own company, Bloom Personal Branding, when I was 45. I provide coaching and training services to entrepreneurs, coaches and business and sales professionals across all walks of life. I may have started a little later than most, but I am okay with that. To me, age is just a number! I am a wife and mother to our beautiful daughter, Mallory—the best job of all! Looking back on my life, I feel like I have accomplished a lot, but I am nowhere near finished. I still have so much to do, and I am so excited about my future.

My bullying experiences also helped me become more aware of how to act and communicate with my daughter. Being a mother is a tremendous responsibility, and it takes effort, patience and grace to raise a confident daughter. I try to be open and approachable, support her passions and encourage her to try new things. I am mindful and careful about what I say about my body, even when I may not like how my jeans fit or how I look in a swimsuit. I try not to be too critical of myself, but especially in front of her. I praise my daughter's positive characteristics, her accomplishments and the hard work and determination she exhibits, so she learns her self-worth isn't tied to her appearance.

Most of all, I am grateful for my self-doubt detox journey of letting go, healing, learning, believing in and loving myself, and taking my power back. I appreciate all the support I received from my husband and daughter, family, friends, mentors, and experts. I am especially thankful to my mother and father, who have always been my biggest cheerleaders.

I know how much COURAGE it takes to start detoxing self-doubt, and I applaud you for starting your journey to beat your bully and bloom confidence! You have made so much progress already by identifying your bully and learning how it negatively impacted your life. The steps I've shared in this book are exactly what I have done to help myself out of self-doubt and to be confident every day. I hope they have helped you realize that you don't want your negative past experiences to define who you are. I hope you want to use them as a source of empowerment to push yourself and to keep trying to achieve your goals. Remember, confidence is a choice. It will take time and hard work to believe in yourself, love yourself and regain your power. Don't give up. You are worth it! You deserve to live your life on your terms.

BLOOM METHODOLOGY KEY TAKEAWAYS

- If you give your power to the bully, the bully always wins. Bullies, no matter who or what they are, deplete your confidence and take away your power. Decide to **own your power** and never give it up.

- Self-Doubt silences your spirit, but don't settle for giving it the last word. If you let your strengths guide you, you will always move in the right direction. Your first step is to **acknowledge** your fears and come to terms with how and why you feel this way.

- **Believe** in yourself. No one else can do this for you. Believing in yourself begins with a shift in your mindset and a change in your attitude to start thinking positively. It's a choice.

- Practicing **loving yourself** every day means choosing to love yourself first. Be kind and give grace to yourself. Learn how to trust yourself with respect. Once you start doing this, you will begin to feel and look at yourself differently. You will feel better.

- You can learn more through **observation** than anything you've ever been told. The power of observation and learning from other people is an ongoing process. Be aware of how confident people look, act and behave. Choose one thing to start with and build from there. Take a small step each week.

- Take advantage of every **opportunity** in life. Opportunities present themselves every day on a small or larger scale. Put yourself out there, try something new and be brave! You may be uncomfortable at first, but the more you become involved in your work, community, hobby, or passion, the more you will fuel your confidence.

- **Mentors** can change your life. Mentors are an integral part of your growth in self-confidence. Don't be afraid to interview that person before you bring him/her into your life. This is the person who will help guide you to your greatness. I believe everyone should have a cheerleader.

Your self-worth comes from truly embracing who you are. Your values, passion and purpose will shine once you learn how to accept yourself.

Resources

I hope we can stay connected on your journey to BLOOM YOUR CONFIDENCE.

Here are some ways:

Visit my website at www.bloompersonalbranding.com for expert and motivational resources to help you look, feel and become a more confident woman.

Join my email newsletter. Send me your email, and I'll add you for a weekly dose of inspiration delivered to your inbox.

Visit www.bloompersonalbranding.com/resources/ for the following:

- To download my freebies:

    21-page Bloom Your Confidence Guidebook
    100 Positive Daily Affirmations to Believe in YOU
    30-Day Self-Love Calendar
    Personal Brand & Image Assessment

- To purchase your "authentically me" white t-shirt.

- To purchase my book for style inspiration – "The Style File—A Woman's Guide to Dress for Success."

🌸 To purchase my eBook: Get Noticed—A 30-Day Plan to Bloom Your Brand

As women, we are part of a special sisterhood because we understand the daily struggles we face. That is why it is important to support each other with encouraging words and acts of kindness. When one woman achieves her goals, it is a win for us all.

If you need support or help understanding your goals and challenges, join my Bloom Your Confidence Membership Community. For a small monthly fee, you can receive group coaching, 1:1 hot seat coaching, courses, tips, strategies, support, guest speakers, and all kinds of inspiration and motivation for your personal growth in my private group community.

To learn more & join, visit www.bloompersonalbranding.com/bloom-your-confidence/

Believe

Love Yourself

Observation

Opportunities

Mentor

Bloom
PERSONAL BRANDING

Made in the USA
Monee, IL
14 March 2024

55041610R00075